Day by Day with God

ROOTING WOMEN'S LIVES IN THE BIBLE

MAY–AUGUST 2006

Christina Press
BRF
Tunbridge Wells/Oxford

Copyright © 2006 Christina Press and BRF

The Bible Reading Fellowship,
First Floor, Elsfield Hall, 15–17 Elsfield Way, Oxford OX2 8FG

First published in Great Britain 2006

ISBN 1 84101 281 5
13-digit ISBN 978 1 84101 281 0

Distributed in Australia by:
Willow Connection, PO Box 288, Brookvale, NSW 2100.
Tel: 02 9948 3957; Fax: 02 9948 8153;
E-mail: info@willowconnection.com.au

Distributed in New Zealand by:
Scripture Union Wholesale, PO Box 760, Wellington
Tel: 04 385 0421; Fax: 04 384 3990;
E-mail: suwholesale@clear.net.nz

Distributed in Canada by:
The Anglican Book Centre, 80 Hayden Street, Toronto, Ontario, M4Y 3G2
Tel: 001 416 924-1332; Fax: 001 416 924-2760;
E-mail: abc@anglicanbookcentre.com; Website: www.anglicanbookcentre.com

Acknowledgments

Printed in Great Britain by Bookmarque, Croydon

Contents

Contributors

Chris Claydon combines her role as a lay reader with pastoral ministry as a vicar's wife. She lived in Israel for seven years, where she developed a contemplative prayer life through teaching and leading retreats.

Chris Leonard is a writer. She has a degree in English and theology and her books range from biography and devotional to children's stories. She enjoys leading creative writing workshops.

Wendy Bray is an award-winning writer and journalist. She has a special interest in faith, life and survivorship issues and runs 'One Life', a personal development and life coaching initiative.

Margaret Killingray works for the London Institute for Contemporary Christianity, where she teaches and writes a weekly email Bible message.

Wendy Virgo is a writer and speaker, travelling widely with her husband Terry, who leads the Newfrontiers family of churches around the world.

Jean Watson's work has included teaching, editing and writing for different age groups and media—books, magazines, radio, TV. She takes in lodgers, runs a small arts group and is a director of a local counselling service.

Fiona Barnard works among international students and researchers in Scotland, and encourages local Christians to reach out in friendship to those temporarily far from home.

Anne Coomes edits a resource website for church magazine editors: Parishpump.co.uk. She is also editor of the inhouse magazines for the Billy Graham Evangelistic Association (UK) and Samaritan's Purse (UK).

Alie Stibbe is a postgraduate student in the Department of Scandinavian Studies at University College, London. She is married to an Anglican minister and they have four children.

Five guest writers have each contributed a one-day focus to this series, to show how God has spoken to them individually through the Bible. They include three writers, **Jane Grayshon**, **Abidemi Sanusi** and **Anne Le Tissier**, Bible teacher **Mo Tizzard**, and youth worker **Caroline Kimber**.

Catherine Butcher writes...

It never ceases to amaze me that the God who made the universe, and maintains its delicate balance, wants to know you and me. Throughout the Bible, God calls people into an intimate relationship with himself: 'You will seek me and find me when you seek me with all your heart. I will be found by you,' God says in Jeremiah 29:13–14.

Throughout this year's Bible reading notes, we are looking particularly at knowing God. In this middle part of the year, Chris Claydon starts off by reminding us how we get to know God in the first place—through his Son, Jesus. To highlight the importance of knowing Jesus, Chris Leonard points to Jesus' contemporaries who missed the opportunity of knowing him. Wendy Bray reminds us of the loving relationship we can have with God, calling him Abba—'daddy'—just as Jesus did.

When Paul met with God in that dramatic encounter on the Damascus road, he was transformed, just as we can be when we know God personally. Margaret Killingray focuses on Paul's life, while Wendy Virgo unpacks one of Paul's great themes: that we know God and reflect God to our world as a community—the body of Christ.

I've been thinking recently about the infinite variety of God's creation and the way he relates to each of us individually, delighting in our uniqueness. Simply sitting in a café on a busy street, watching all the people passing by, we can see all sizes, shapes and ages; various colours and complexions; each one made in God's image. Human systems so often offer sameness, not variety; mono, not multicolour. God's ways are often not our ways of thinking or living. Jean Watson helps us to look at life from a different perspective—living on the edge, where we can learn so much from the contrasting circumstances we face: joy and sorrow, living and dying, looking back and looking forward.

As the summer holiday season starts, we turn to look at David, the shepherd king, who knew God in a special way. Fiona Barnard starts by looking at David's life, then Anne Coomes and Alie Stibbe take us into the Psalms to learn more about God and how to live in his presence.

The last five days of August offer something completely different: five Christian women share a passage of scripture that God has used to speak to them at a particular point in their lives.

As you use these notes, ask God to speak to you individually through the Bible passages and through the comments made by our contributors.

An invitation we can't refuse!

[Two disciples followed Jesus.] Turning round, Jesus saw them following and asked, 'What do you want?' They said, 'Rabbi' (which means Teacher), 'where are you staying?' 'Come', he replied, 'and you will see.'

There's a thread running through this first week of this new series about knowing God, which, I trust will help us to know him more closely; and the thread is the word 'come'. The invitation in today's reading comes from the lips of Jesus. What a wonderful invitation it was then for those disciples who were following, and still is for us today as we follow him in 2006. As we respond with a glad affirmative, we can look forward to deepening encounters, face to face with him.

Do you remember, as a child at school, when invitations were being given out for a birthday celebration? It was such a joy when you were included and such a feeling of being an outsider when you were not. It was partly seeing the friend's home and meeting her parents that moved your friendship to a deeper level, and of course eating together!

Well, the disciples on this occasion knew that Jesus was a rabbi, a teacher of the Hebrew scriptures, but they didn't know Jesus personally as a friend. Picture the scene as they followed him that day, probably at a respectful distance, and Jesus turning round and taking the initiative, 'What do you want?' I'm sure they were caught off guard and blurted out: 'Where are you staying?' The invitation to come and see led to an experience that would change the rest of their lives.

At which point are you in your relationship with Jesus? Has he passed by, perhaps years ago? Do you believe that he knows you are following, but at a distance? It is possible that he is turning round and inviting you to come closer and spend quality time with him, to hear him speak as you read his word in the coming weeks.

....

'Look at me. I stand at the door. I knock. If you hear me call and open the door, I'll come right in and sit down to supper with you' (Revelation 3:20, THE MESSAGE). Think of these words as an invitation to you. What is your response?

CC

Jesus... still calling

Walking along the beach of Lake Galilee, Jesus saw two brothers: Simon (later called Peter), and Andrew. They were fishing, throwing their nets into the lake. It was their regular work. Jesus said to them, 'Come with me, and I'll make a new kind of fisherman out of you.'

I have had the privilege of living in Israel for several years, and a favourite spot for me was by the shore of Galilee, near Capernaum, where I'd sit and listen to the waves lapping on the shingle... can you hear it? I once taped that sound for an aunt of mine, who had very poor vision, and the sound of the waves and the gulls helped her to imagine a passage, such as this, very vividly.

Well, I hope you are there, too, and can imagine Jesus striding up to the fishermen who were casting their nets. Jesus didn't wait to draw up a contract, but he saw the potential of these men and offered them 'cabinet posts' on the spot! Soon after, he also called James and John, their business partners, and the four made a trustworthy core/foundation group to the twelve who gathered round Jesus for the next three years.

I think we can be fairly sure that they had met Jesus before; perhaps further south where John the Baptist had been baptizing people in the river Jordan, somewhere near Jerusalem. God had gone before and prepared the way in their hearts, minds and spirits. A routine day's fishing provided a close encounter that they hadn't bargained for, and that changed the rest of their lives! It involved a response from each named individual Jesus spoke to. They didn't ask questions, but simply dropped their nets and followed him.

As you go about your 'regular work', be it within the home or outside of it, Jesus may surprise you with a close encounter that might involve a response that will change your approach to the rest of your life. Looking back we can often see that God has been preparing us 'for such a time as this'.

....

Listen for Jesus' call to you through this word of scripture, and make your response immediately.

Read about Matthew's own surprising call in Luke 5:27–32.

CC

Too busy?

The apostles then rendezvoused with Jesus and reported on all that they had done and taught. Jesus said, 'Come off by yourselves; let's take a break and get a little rest.'

The backdrop for writing this note was a brilliant sunshine day at Whiting Bay on the Isle of Arran in Scotland. Under a cloudless blue sky, the sea was aqua blue, shading in the deeper water to indigo/purple. Small wavelets were coming up the shingle shore with white, lacy edges, and the sounds were rhythmical, like breathing out and breathing in. I realized that each water particle was being reabsorbed into the depths where it was revitalized before returning to the shore in shining glory.

This seems to be the pattern for Jesus' life as he lived on earth; he spent early mornings, or whole nights, with his heavenly Father and then was refreshed to meet with the crowds again for teaching and healing. It is not surprising, therefore, to find him helping his disciples into the same rhythm, as we see in these verses. The apostles/disciples had been in the villages, teaching and healing. Then they returned to report to Jesus, and he encouraged them to take a break with him and get rested, before beginning again.

Jesus' experience of being *incarnate* (i.e. fully God and fully man) meant that he experienced and understood the hazard of fatigue and the danger of what we call today 'burn-out'. I'm sure he would encourage us to live with the same rhythm that he practised and that he encouraged his first disciples to practise. Many people find it a help to go away for a day, or even a weekend, to be on their own without distraction and listen to God through his word. It might be possible to enlist the help of an experienced Christian if this would be a 'first'.

Too busy? A suggestion: a guided retreat might help. Take time to reflect on these words from Matthew 11:28–30 (*THE MESSAGE*).

....

'Are you tired? Worn out? Burned out on religion? Come to me. Get away with me and you'll recover your life. I'll show you how to take a real rest. Walk with me and work with me—watch how I do it… Keep company with me and you'll learn to live freely and lightly.'

CC

Honest questions

Nicodemus… came to Jesus at night and said, 'Rabbi, we know you are a teacher who has come from God… In reply Jesus declared, 'I tell you the truth, no one can see the kingdom of God without being born again.'

The Pharisees were a leading group of Jews who lived strictly by every detail of the law of Moses and were obsessed with making sure that others did the same. Nicodemus came to Jesus when no one could see him, especially not fellow Pharisees; remember, there were no street lights 2,000 years ago! Jesus must have recognized his earnest desire to talk, though Nicodemus didn't recognize the deeper truths as yet. Honest questions are the starting point for some, often at night. Jesus' answers may surprise us!

Have you ever listened to a piece of music and heard at first the melody, and then later the harmonies of other instruments, and been enriched by the whole spectrum of the composer's creation? Well, Jesus took this Pharisee from his initial observation that Jesus was a rabbi, into the depths of understanding that would change his whole life radically.

We are focusing in the coming weeks on knowing God more closely, and more deeply, so be prepared for some surprises. It may be that you are following Jesus unbeknown to family and friends; or that you have questions still needing an answer. Wherever you are on your spiritual journey, you can be confident that as you encounter Jesus day by day, he will draw you closer to him.

This talk that Nicodemus had with Jesus was not the end of the story, for we meet him again three years later at the time of Jesus' crucifixion, when he helped to carry Jesus' lifeless body to the tomb. He provided an amazing quantity of spices, such as would only be used for royal burials. Nicodemus had understood Jesus' teaching about being born again, and had allowed it to transform his life.

....

Day by day, dear Lord, of thee three things I pray: to see thee more clearly, to love thee more dearly, follow thee more nearly, day by day.
Sir Richard of Chichester (1197–1253)

A surprisingly close encounter!

Zacchaeus... wanted to see who Jesus was, but being a short man he could not, because of the crowd. So he ran ahead and climbed a sycamore-fig tree to see him... When Jesus reached the spot, he looked up and said to him, 'Zacchaeus, come down immediately. I must stay at your house today.'

Recently the Queen visited Colchester and a friend of mine wanted to see her, so she got up early and took up her position near the town hall steps so that she could be sure of a clear sighting. It was well worth the wait as she was able to give the Queen the flowers that she had brought and heard her speak.

Zacchaeus truly wanted to see Jesus, but probably had no greater expectation than that. I'm sure that what followed in the next hour or so had not, even faintly, crossed his mind. He just wanted a good view and to be hidden from the unwanted attention of those who would abuse him as a tax-collector. (Note: tax-collectors were Jews working for the Romans, and therefore thought to be traitors. They were known to demand more money than they should and grew wealthy as a result. No wonder they were not top of the popularity polls!)

When Jesus reached 'the spot', the very tree that Zacchaeus had climbed a few hours earlier, he looked up. I wonder if Zacchaeus, being a short man, and generally despised, had ever had the experience of someone looking up at him. Then, as if that was not enough, came the request by Jesus to visit his home, then and there. Zacchaeus had not just a sighting, but a close encounter that changed his way of life for ever: 'Today is salvation-day in this home' (THE MESSAGE).

It is just the same today, when we move from seeing Jesus on the printed page, to knowing him in our life, in our home, in our spirit. When we encounter him in prayer, then it is the same for us more than 2000 years later.

....

Recall to mind an occasion when you made a tremendous effort to see someone you admired, and were rewarded with more than a sighting! Ask for God's help as you draw closer to Jesus.

CC

Seriously thirsty

Jesus stood and said in a loud voice, 'Let anyone who is thirsty come to me and drink. Whoever believes in me, as the Scripture has said, will have streams of living water flowing from within.'

Can you remember a time in your life when you were seriously thirsty? Spend a moment reliving that occasion. I am remembering a time when I was sitting with a friend in the driver's cab of a lorry by the river Niger, waiting for the Jebba bridge to clear so that we could drive on south. We both had babies on our knees, our water bottles were lukewarm, and suddenly, out of the blue, an arm shot through the open window clutching two bottles of ice-cold Coke! No drink has ever been so amazing.

These sorts of memories bring to life the dramatic statement of Jesus during a Jewish festival, when many were gathered in the temple precincts in Jerusalem. Those who heard would be familiar with the words from the prophet Isaiah: 'Come, all who are thirsty, come to the waters…' They would know that he was not referring to literal water, but to the quenching of a thirst of the spirit.

Jesus once met a woman by a well. She had come to draw water and Jesus also was tired and thirsty. She was not aware of who it was she was meeting, but he knew all about her; as he knows about us. He introduced her to the water of the Spirit in these words: 'Everyone who drinks this (well) water will be thirsty again, but whoever drinks the water I give them will never thirst. Indeed, the water I give will become a spring of water welling up to eternal life' (John 4:6–14).

Jesus is still offering us this most refreshing, life-restoring water, as we draw close to him.

Let us drink deeply from the spring of living water.

Find the water of life wonderfully described in Revelation 22:1–6 and 17.

CC

The phone rings; it's nearly midnight; I'm already drifting off to sleep. Drowsily, I answer.

'It's me,' says a dejected voice (when you're close to someone, two words are enough to give instant recognition, especially when you're expecting to hear from them). 'I've missed the train!'

Living at the end of the line, when missing the last train from London means there's no other way home, phone calls like this leave a helpless, empty, disappointed feeling. Even without words, the dejected voice means he's feeling the same. But it's not the end of the world. There's another train tomorrow morning. A colleague has a spare room where he can stay the night. It simply means more time apart. Less time tomorrow to enjoy each other's company. It's a consequence of our own choice to live 100 miles away from his work in northwest London, so we can bring up our children in a town near the sea and South Downs rather than the bustling metropolis.

Choices mean consequences. Some choices are almost meaningless: margarine or butter; with or without milk; we make millions of choices in life. But some choices are crucial: choosing to say 'Yes' when I hear God calling me. Choosing to take time to get to know him. Choosing to live God's way, not my own way.

Jesus talked to his closest friends about choices that would make a vital difference—because there would be an end of the world, when choices would have consequences. Sheep, goats, talents and wedding attendants all tumble together in Matthew 25 where Jesus talked to his disciples about the end of time: 'When the Son of Man comes in his glory, and all the angels with him... All the nations will be gathered before him...'

That's when I want to be sure I've not missed the opportunity to know Jesus; I want to be among those who will hear his voice saying: 'Come, you who are blessed by my Father; take your inheritance, the kingdom prepared for you since the creation of the world...'

Don't miss the opportunities he gives you to get to know him better.

People who missed knowing Jesus

'I will judge you by your own words, you wicked servant! You knew, did you, that I am a hard man, taking out what I did not put in, and reaping what I did not sow?'

We have just been exploring some basics of getting to know Jesus. For the next couple of weeks let's turn that upside down and inside out, coming at it from a different angle. Have you ever wondered about all those who actually met the man Jesus, yet never got to know him? Or why people of his own day acted or reacted in ways that prevented them from knowing him better? The third servant in today's parable, for example, seemed too terrified to invest what he'd been left. Why? Because he had failed to understand his master's nature. A fictional character, of course, he couldn't have met Jesus. But Jesus told his story as a wake-up call for real people like him... or like us, perhaps.

Do you know anyone so afraid of displeasing their hard, exacting 'God' that they won't take the risks required in following Jesus? Maybe that's why I don't take the opportunity to share my faith sometimes. I'm bound to mess it up. Safer to leave it to someone else!

If, like that servant, I think of God as mean and vengeful rather than generous and full of grace, I'll miss knowing Jesus better—and miss all the excitement of working with him. How would I ever dare act as his hands and feet on this earth?

Let us see what we can learn from those who failed, in some measure, to know Jesus. (There are so many that we'll limit ourselves to Luke's Gospel.) Sounds depressing? The encouraging thing shouting from almost every page of the Bible is that failure's no problem to God. Interim school-type reports on most Bible characters would read, 'Could do better.' Most did, with God's grace, do much 'better', as they dared to know him better.

....

Ask God to open your mind, heart, spirit, attitudes and behaviour to different ways in which you might come to know Jesus better.

Read Romans 8:1–2 to boost your confidence in the grace of God.

CL

Unbelief

Zechariah said to the angel, 'Do you expect me to believe this? I'm an old man and my wife is an old woman.' But the angel said, '… because you won't believe me, you'll be unable to say a word until the day of your son's birth.'

In a riveting family saga outshining any TV soap or reality show, an angel tells two different people of their respective parts in supernatural births that are about to happen. They react to this high drama in similar ways. Mary asks the angel, 'But how? I've never slept with a man.' She gets a straight answer—as straight as is possible to any question about the mystery of the incarnation.

The response to Zechariah's question, by contrast, is to be struck dumb for not believing the angel's words. Why? He 'enjoyed a clear conscience before God'. He'd been praying, for the angel greeted him with the words, 'Don't fear, Zechariah, your prayer has been heard. Elizabeth, your wife, will bear a son by you.'

Zechariah's miracle isn't as 'way out' as Mary's. The only other difference I can see is that Mary believes that this thing will be and merely asks how. Zechariah doesn't believe. He wants a sign—and gets one. Imagine receiving news like that and then not being able to speak for months! All is not lost, despite his cynicism. As soon as his tongue is released he's pouring forth praise and faith. During that silent time the old man had come to know God better.

God has no problem with our asking him questions. But perhaps there is something wrong with praying when we're convinced that the answer's impossible for God—especially if he desires the same thing, for purposes greater than our own selfish ones! Mature, worshipping, interceding Christian women can make that mistake just as easily as an elderly Jewish priest. Ever been shocked dumb at his answer? I've certainly been surprised when, had I known him better, I shouldn't have been.

....

Help us to learn to pray in faith, Lord, and keep us from unbelief when you pour out your goodness on us.

CL

Familiarity

His parents were not impressed; they were upset and hurt. His mother said, 'Young man, why have you done this to us?' ... 'No prophet is ever welcomed in his hometown.'

Jesus is a challenge. Foolishly, sometimes I think I know and understand him. Ha! I'd be frantic if a twelve-year-old of mine went absent-without-leave for three days, even (especially?) if I discovered that he'd been at some Bible camp, teaching the nation's foremost Christian leaders. Jesus appears to make no allowances for his mother's point of view, or for poor Joseph's position as an odd kind of stepfather when he asks, 'Why were you looking for me? Didn't you know I had to be here, dealing with the things of my Father?' They didn't understand. Jesus didn't enlighten them further.

Just when we think we're most familiar with Jesus, sometimes he proves the most difficult to know. Imagine someone you'd known in your neighbourhood since he was tiny. He moved away. Later there were rumours of miracles. Then he marches into your church, bold as anything, claiming to be God's special anointed one. Won't everyone be asking, 'But isn't that old Joe's son?'

After their natural-sounding question, Jesus launches a fierce attack on the villagers, provoking their attempt to murder him. Previously I've misread the passage, thinking the people of Nazareth taunted Jesus with, 'Doctor, go heal yourself.' But those words are in Jesus' mouth. Unfortunately, this isn't on film. We can't see the villagers' faces, or hear music suggestive of a poisonous atmosphere building.

Familiarity bred contempt in Nazareth. Even his mother failed to know her twelve-year-old son as Lord. If we are to get to know Jesus we have to understand that his ways are not our ways. Draw encouragement though, that Mary stayed with him at the cross and that she, and Jesus' brother James strengthened the early church.

....

Lord, may I never replace you with some familiar, comfortable 'Jesus' I've constructed. May I follow you, even when I don't understand.

Read Luke 8:19–21 for another example. Does it teach or encourage you?

CL

Distracted

**Martha was distracted by all the preparations that had to be made…
'Lord, don't you care that my sister has left me to do the work by
myself? Tell her to help me!'**

What distracts you from getting to know Jesus better? This morning I
tried to sit down and simply be with him. Not praying, not praising,
not confessing, just being with him, making myself available should he
want to say anything. I made myself comfortable, had pen and paper
handy on which to jot down and put aside all the 'urgent' things that
normally spring to mind on such occasions. I set the kitchen timer—
five minutes should be do-able. But, when it bleeped, my thoughts
were not with Jesus. They'd been round the world a few times.

I tried again, with marginally more success. After all, when getting
to know anyone, it's much better to spend time with them on their
terms than to do all the talking. And spending time with Jesus is such
a privilege. If he turned up at our house, I think I would sit at his feet,
aware that the reason for his visit would hardly be my superlative
housewife skills. As it is, I can easily ignore him in preparing for things
I have to do. Which is why I need to practise being in his presence.

Read Jesus' explanation of his 'sower' story in Luke 8:11–15. Think
about the distractions there. Jesus said the good seed was the word of
God.

Many words are thrown at us every day. Do they distract us from
the truth found in scripture, the 'now' words God has given us, the
Word himself? They say a family tragedy either strengthens a marriage
or precipitates divorce, depending on attitude. What's your reaction
towards Jesus in times of crisis? What distracts you from him normally—worries, riches, pleasures… something else?

All relationships of any depth need time and attention—and, as distractions are everywhere, an honest review from time to time.

....

*A great mystery: despite the
Lord's countless relationships,
and our own behaviour, he's
never distracted from any of us!*

Read John 11:1–45 and 12:2
for encouragement about how
Martha's relationship with Jesus
grew.

CL

Materialism

'That's what happens when you fill your barn with Self and not with God... Steep yourself in God-reality, God-initiative, God-provisions. You'll find all your everyday human concerns will be met.'

What might you have first said to Jesus? Hopefully not: 'Order my brother to give me a fair share of the family inheritance!' Jesus soon revealed what lay behind the question—greed. It's hard to enjoy a rich relationship with God if material things fill your mind. We don't hear again of the man who asked the question. Mere money appears to have kept him from a prime opportunity to know Jesus.

Obsession with material things is especially common among the very rich—or the very poor. Nearly all the people of Jesus' day were one or the other. What with Roman taxes, temple taxes and inherited land taken from them, most, including carpenters, lived well below the breadline. If you and your family are hungry, you'll be working all hours, desperate to keep everyone alive. In theory God may be with you, but it's not easy to put him first.

A few of Jesus' countrymen exploited the situation, siding with Herod or the Romans, becoming rich—though not towards God or their compatriots. Where I live, wealth is spread more evenly, yet we can drown in all the financial information that comes, usually uninvited, into our homes. Pensions, investments, credit cards, all with their small print, all horribly complex and worrying.

But can we rely on God alone? Interesting that this passage says God supplies what we need—not what we want, or think we need. Foxes have holes, the birds their nests, but even Jesus didn't always have somewhere to lay his head. Being 'full of God' doesn't mean being comfortable. He may ask us to give away what we do have. On the other hand, missing knowing Jesus because of greed, or worry about material things, is tragic.

Ask God to help you to recognize your heart attitude to possessions—and take time to respond as necessary.

Read the Ten Commandments (Exodus 20:1–17) to see what light they throw on relationships with God and people.

CL

Self-sufficient, safe, indifferent

'But woe to you who are rich, for you have already received your comfort... who are well fed now, for you will go hungry... who laugh now, for you will mourn and weep... when everyone speaks well of you, for that is how their ancestors treated the false prophets.'

You and I may not be 'Bill Gates rich' but we're unimaginably rich compared with most people in the world. Most of us live in reasonable comfort and don't go to bed hungry, unless by choice. We're probably happy to be respectable, well thought of, well liked.

Jesus' commands, which follow this uncomfortable passage, seem almost impossible to fulfil. Such extreme forgiveness, such extreme generosity—extremism in any form confronts my safe self-sufficiency which, I like to think, never hurt anyone.

And so, unwilling to squander time or money, I go on shopping at the most convenient supermarket for the best-value goods. I'm not giving everything to the poor—I'd become a burden on others. I'm surprised, not altogether unpleasantly, when people think what a good person I must be to write Bible notes. Yet millions of people across the world are dying for want of food, clean water, medicine. Passages like this make me wonder if I know—or depend on—Jesus at all.

I read my church home group the words of 'Crumbs from your table' (from U2's 2004 album *How to Dismantle an Atomic Bomb*). Bono's incandescent anger at American evangelicals' indifference to the plight of dying Africans challenged us. If we say we know Jesus, but ignore the 2103 scriptures about caring for the poor, why would anyone believe us, let alone believe in him? Then a group member told us about working for one of the many Christian relief and development organizations that *are* making a difference.

....

You challenge, not to condemn but that we might know you better, Lord. Show me how I might imagine with you a renewed world— and work with you to see it happen.

CL

Ungenerous

The older brother became angry and refused to go in. So his father went out and pleaded with him... He answered... 'Look! All these years I've been slaving for you and never disobeyed your orders. Yet you never gave me even a young goat so I could celebrate with my friends.'

I write books. If someone at one of the creative writing courses I run announced she'd received a £1 million advance for her blockbuster novel, I'd react with delight—probably. But if I judged my writing much better than hers, my sweet 'Babycham' smiles might disguise the sour grapes of indignation.

Jesus told this story to society's outcasts, to obvious sinners who fed on his every word, while religious types stood to one side, muttering disapproval. As stories go, it was pretty pointed. The younger son, having treated his father as if dead, indulged in wild living, then slummed it alongside that Jewish taboo, the pig. Yet, on his return, his father laid on the most lavish party—just as Jesus embraced, ate and spent time with dishonest, promiscuous, exploitative no-gooders. If, like the hard-working older son in the story, those who read the scriptures, obeyed God's law, prayed, worked and worshipped, ended up on the outside, it wasn't Jesus who pushed them there. While 'ordinary' people sought him out, the ungenerous spirits of many morally upright, religious people sidelined them away from the party, trapped in an indignant sulk.

Like the older son, they never understood that their Father would have given them a 'party' any time they wanted. The truth is that no one, however religious or good, deserves God's favour. His grace is outrageous. Yet somehow we give the impression that the main thing about Christianity is being perfect. Many 'ordinary people' think a Christian is someone who's 'goody-goody' or self-righteous. It keeps them from knowing Jesus—when the truth is, we're all a mess, in need of grace.

....

How do people react if an adulterer, drug-user or ex-prisoner turns up in your church? How would Jesus react?

CL

19

Politically correct

A religious scholar stood up with a question to test Jesus. 'Teacher, what do I need to do to get eternal life?' He answered, 'What's written in God's Law? How do you interpret it?'

Luke 9:52–53 mentions that a Samaritan village did not welcome Jesus 'because his destination was Jerusalem'. Samaria was the spiritual and political capital of a breakaway kingdom formed by ten of Israel's tribes. The remaining tribes of Judah and Benjamin formed the kingdom of Judah and worshipped at the Jerusalem temple. Each dismissed the other as wrong. The Samaritan villagers, convinced their own religion and politics were right, labelled Jesus one of the 'others'—and missed knowing him. Protestant, Roman Catholic, Orthodox, Reformed, Liberal… religious fractures below today's political fault-lines can release earthquake-like mayhem. Even in quieter times, they prevent many from knowing Jesus.

Jesus' 'good Samaritan' story gives a further twist. The religious scholar in Jerusalem already knew the correct answer to the question he asked—to love God with everything you've got and your neighbour as much as yourself. So why did he miss knowing Jesus? Luke says he wanted to justify himself (NIV). Did he really think he could do all that loving without help? Possibly. Did he think he knew better than this 'young upstart', Jesus? Probably, because Jesus answered his question with a story revealing the scholar's thinking to be completely wrong. It was a bit like pointing out to an evangelical leader that God thought a Mormon or Jehovah's Witness was doing better than him.

The story teaches us that eternal life—a lasting relationship with God, following Jesus—isn't for the politically, or religiously, correct. We're all flawed, whether or not our sin is socially acceptable. Political or religious correctness allows no room for the amazement that is grace. Only God's grace allows us to love God, and our neighbour, fully.

....

Race, religion, prejudice, history—if nothing separates us from God's love (Romans 8:39), surely we can't let these things separate us from loving the people he made!

CL

Rigidity, ingratitude

One of them, when he realized that he was healed, turned around and came back... kneeled at Jesus' feet, so grateful. He couldn't thank him enough—and he was a Samaritan.

It was important to God-fearing Jews from the northern 'Galilee of the Gentiles' to make the three great festival pilgrimages south to the Jerusalem temple each year. The easiest route lay through hostile land, which must have been hard for them. Luke says that when Jesus travelled to Jerusalem on this occasion he took a route along the border between Samaria and Galilee. I pay attention when the Bible mentions borders. Some fence people in or out for good reasons. Others need to be crossed, though the crossing takes courage.

Whether we have an official membership list or not, we tend to draw borders around our churches. Who is in? Who an outsider? People can't belong before they believe the right things, conform to the correct behaviour—or can they? Outsiders often responded to Jesus with gratitude. Being grateful to someone deepens your relationship, warms it. Ingratitude does the opposite; it hardens the heart as people become convinced that good things come as of right.

Only one of the ten lepers that Jesus healed came back. All would have been outsiders in the sense that their contagious disease kept them away from their families and communities. Healed, they had years of catching up to do! Yet the Samaritan's first reaction was 'to praise God in a loud voice'. Then he threw himself at Jesus' feet, his gratitude extravagant to the point of worship—decidedly un-PC for his race. Jesus, who wouldn't be hemmed in by borders, treated all ten from the start as 'belonging' and commended the Samaritan for his faith. The others were healed, but missed out, crossing a lesser boundary than the Samaritan negotiated. One day, all had to cross death's boundary but, so far as we know, only the Samaritan got to know Jesus first.

....

Can you throw yourself in grati-tude at Jesus' feet, without any sense of boundary, or rigidity? Do you need to ask him to soften your heart first?

Use a psalm like Psalm 138 to praise God.

CL

Status and power

A dispute arose among them as to which of them was considered to be greatest. Jesus said to them, 'The kings of the Gentiles lord it over them... you are not to be like that. Instead... the one who rules [should be] like the one who serves.'

Have you ever come straight from a particularly holy moment when you met with God, at church perhaps, only to snap over a child's clumsy action back home? Or run down an individual's effort at leading the church service? I have. Jesus' slow-to-learn disciples had several disputes about which of them was greatest. This particular one arose, of all times, straight after the Last Supper. They had been wondering about which of them would betray Jesus. You might say they all did, as I do.

And yet, in the next breath Jesus was commending these same bickering, power-hungry men because they stood by him in his trials. He even promised them a kingdom where they would sit on twelve thrones, judging the tribes of Israel! Just as he continues to invite me, and you, to serve alongside him, to share in his sorrows and joys and, eventually, to rule with him too. 'If we endure, we will also reign with him,' says 2 Timothy 2:12. The hard lessons we learn walking with him on this earth help transform us so we can 'reign' in a godly way.

Right from the beginning, God created people to rule over the earth—not to dominate and enslave but, by serving, to empower, facilitating growth and fruitfulness. Before Jesus' crucifixion, resurrection and ascension, before the Spirit came into their very hearts to teach them all things, the disciples continually missed understanding Jesus. They found it especially hard to comprehend the way he exercised authority, his attitude to his own status and that of others. Later they did learn to serve, to the point of giving their lives. Unlike them in the early days, we don't have the excuse of living pre-resurrection—but God's grace remains the same.

....

When you're in a position of authority, ask God to help you find Jesus there, so you use your authority according to his ways.

Read Luke 9:46–48 and ask God what you can learn from children about not missing Jesus.

CL

Playing safe

'New wine must be poured into new wineskins. And none of you, after drinking old wine, wants the new, for you say, "The old is better."'

It has taken me years to get my head around this one. My heart still lags behind. After all, old wine is better—normally. Surely Jesus isn't advocating following the old ways rather than his new gospel?

John the Baptist's disciples (old wine) took righteous living seriously, fasting and praying. Jesus' disciples ate, drank and often got things wrong. Jesus himself ate and drank with low-life who dishonestly extorted money from their own impoverished people. He forgave their sins. Shocking—only God could do that!

To respectable religious types, Jesus' new wine appeared, not better, but dangerous. 'Don't try it!' they said to themselves—and others. Would I have tried it? Probably not until it had 'matured' a bit, calmed down, become less wild, less messy. (New wine goes to the head quicker than old.) I fear, had I lived in the first century, I might well have avoided 'drinking' it—getting to know Jesus better. Now of course the wine of the gospel has matured, become less dangerous. We have special chalices, and places in which to sip it in a quiet, holy atmosphere.

But supposing the wine that is Jesus keeps being made new? Supposing it's still fizzing and fermenting and bursting out of whatever container you put it in—a chalice or church building, for example, or the accepted way of doing something? Supposing it wants to be medicine for the unclean and impure, the sick and dying? Supposing it becomes wildly intoxicating, like the 'best wine' into which Jesus transformed huge amounts of water as a 'sign to reveal his glory'. It was then, at that Cana wedding, when 'his disciples put their faith in him' according to John 2:11. Ephesians 5:18 advises getting intoxicated with the Spirit. Playing safe isn't compatible with knowing Jesus.

....

Read John 2:1–11, see yourself in the crowd and ask Jesus how he would have wanted you to react. Then ask him to show you similar scenarios in your life today.

CL

Too arrogant for grace

'She was forgiven many, many sins and so she is very, very grateful. If the forgiveness is minimal, the gratitude is minimal.'

Sometimes, reading stories like this, I half-wish I'd done some of the more spectacular sins: adultery, drugs, murder… Daft. If I want to be forgiven much, and therefore love much, I've only to confess my more intransigent sins like pride, worry, independence, self-centredness, unforgiveness, bitterness…

Wouldn't you think that inviting a man around for a meal would be a good way to get to know him? But that didn't seem to be Simon the Pharisee's motivation. He invited Jesus to dinner and then really was very rude to him. Even before the woman's behaviour affronted Simon, he offered Jesus none of the common courtesies that hosts extended to welcome guests in those days.

If the poor in spirit are blessed, Simon was cursed. He believed, having all the right credentials before God, he didn't need Jesus. He was probably hoping to catch him out. And the way Jesus let that 'loose woman' behave, it looked as though he had. Except that she did all the things that Simon, as host, should have done. Plus she understood Jesus better than Simon did—and knew herself better than Simon knew himself. Had she met Jesus before, 'offstage' from Luke's account? Had he extended forgiveness to her then? Or had word simply got around that he would forgive sinners such as herself? Interesting that sin isn't the barrier between us and God. Self-righteousness is. Spiritual arrogance is. Judging—and not forgiving—others is.

The woman left with Jesus' blessing of peace ringing in her ears. Simon must have felt anything but wholeness, peace, 'shalom'. His dinner party was ruined, his rudeness revealed to all. Worse, in accepting no grace from his guest, Simon missed an amazing opportunity to get to know Jesus. In opposing Jesus, he brought judgment on himself.

....

God's opposition to the proud and grace towards the humble threads right through scripture—check it out!

Read 1 Peter 5:5–6 (which doesn't apply only to 'young men'!).

CL

Good or evil?

Jesus was driving out a demon that was mute... the crowd was amazed. But some of them said, 'By Beelzebub, the prince of demons, he is driving out demons.'

Saying that Jesus' power and good actions come from the devil pushes failure to get to know him to extremes. If 'the light within you' is darkness (v. 34), that's serious. In Matthew's parallel passage Jesus says, 'Anyone who speaks a word against the Son of Man will be forgiven, but anyone who speaks against the Holy Spirit will not be forgiven, either in this age or in the age to come' (Matthew 12:32). We need to be careful about what we call 'evil' or 'of the devil'.

I am still reeling from a discussion the other night when a Christian woman insisted that any attempt to help the world's poor, whether through aid, debt relief or fair trade, only makes matters worse—multiplies evil: that the poor deserve their sickness and misery, deserve their children to die. No! Her assertions might find echoes in the Hindu doctrine of karma but are completely alien to the whole of scripture and to the personality of the Holy Spirit.

God's grace-dynamic renews hope, causing us to imagine and set in motion a new start. He commands and empowers us to drive out evil, harmful influences as Jesus did, to liberate God's ability to love in those who give and those who receive. If people say that is wrong, their light is indeed darkness. I'm not saying this woman committed the unforgivable sin but such reversal of good and evil is serious.

There were no letters 30 metres high proclaiming 'Behold God's work!' in Jesus' day and there certainly aren't now. Unlike Jesus, some of the people who are acting in his name won't be perfect. Like Jesus, they will come across corruption. Evil won't lie down and die quietly. There will be a cost. Be realistic, but never cynical. Be on the side of hope and of the (good) angels!

···

Don't miss God's goodness. Ask God to reveal cynicism in your heart.

Meditate on Psalm 36:9—and allow God's life and light to sink into your heart.

CL

Failing to recognize Jesus

As they talked and discussed these things with each other, Jesus himself came up and walked along with them; but they were kept from recognizing him.

These two disciples did know Jesus, so what kept them from recognizing him? Shock and grief over the recent death of their beloved Master meant that they weren't functioning properly. They'd thought he would save them: now everything had turned dark, no wonder they couldn't see.

Hindsight is a fine thing. I can look back over all kinds of circumstances that I railed against, rather than recognizing Jesus at work in them. But, having spent fourteen days considering people in Luke who missed knowing Jesus, I find this story encouraging. Jesus takes such care to explain things, even though his disciples treat him as an ignorant outsider. They sound increasingly affronted, telling their side of the story. But when Jesus unpacks scripture, their hearts 'burn within them'. They are hanging on his every word. On reaching their destination they don't know yet that it is him but they do know that this stranger has the words of life. They don't want him to leave.

I don't suppose any of us could get to know even a fraction of Jesus all at once. We see and begin to know different aspects of him in different circumstances. On their *Glo* album, the band Delirious? sings about an 'Intimate Stranger'—an appropriate title not just at Emmaus but for one who still reveals different aspects of himself in different situations and guises. Often when we ourselves fail to get things right, fail to recognize him, fail to follow or to be like him—that's when that 'Stranger', he who searched for one lost sheep, bends down and gently picks us up. 'He tends his flock like a shepherd: He gathers the lambs in his arms and carries them close to his heart; he gently leads those that have young' (Isaiah 40:11).

....

So often we miss knowing you properly, Lord. That's when you gather us up. Bring our hearts and minds and souls and strength back to loving you!

Meditate on John 10:1–16 to learn more about the 'knowing' between sheep and shepherd.

CL

In the narrow streets of middle-eastern cities like Jerusalem there are hundreds of doors and gates, some leading into tiny homes, some to shady courtyard gardens, some right through the ancient walls which surround the city. The size of the door gives little indication of what's on the other side or who can go through. Some give access to all, even if they're still riding a camel; others are small making access less easy. Some are open arches; others require a key if they are to be opened.

Jesus sometimes used doors and gates as illustrations when he was explaining to his disciples how they could relate to God. Once, someone asked him, 'Lord, are only a few people going to be saved?' As usual he did not give a straight answer, but said to them, 'Make every effort to enter through the narrow door... Once the owner of the house gets up and closes the door, you will stand outside knocking and pleading, "Sir, open the door for us." But he will answer, "I don't know you or where you come from."

'Then you will say, "We ate and drank with you, and you taught in our streets."

'But he will reply, "I don't know you..."' (Luke 13:23–27).

How tragic, to have spent time 'with' Jesus, but for him to say 'I don't know you...'

Sometimes when I have a house full of guests and I'm busy catering, the door closes at the end of the evening and I realize I've spent hours 'with' my guests, but have been so busy I've not had time to get to know any of them any better. It can be like that with God, which is especially tragic as he sent Jesus so we could get to know him intimately. Jesus said plainly that God operates an open-door policy: 'knock and the door will be opened to you' (Matthew 7:7).

Jesus also explained: 'I am the gate; whoever enters through me will be saved' (John 10:9), and he promised: 'In my Father's house are many rooms; if it were not so, I would have told you. I am going there to prepare a place for you' (John 14:2).

Do you spend time doing 'God's work' while missing the opportunity to know him? As Chris Leonard has shown, even in Jesus' day some were too proud, too busy, too rich. Try using the lighter May mornings (in the northern hemisphere) to wake up a little earlier and start the habit of spending time getting to know God better.

What's in a name?

For to us a child is born, to us a son is given, and the government will be on his shoulders. And he will be called Wonderful Counsellor, Mighty God, Everlasting Father, Prince of Peace.

Most of us will be known by more than one 'title': sister, friend, colleague, mum, wife, deacon—perhaps all six. Captain of the tennis club, godmother, nursing sister, champion rally driver or master acrobat. OK—my imagination is stretching! But it's a useful exercise to list all the 'titles' by which we are known. Exhausting perhaps, but life-affirming!

God also has a wealth of titles as varied as the many aspects of his character. God as Father is the title we are probably most familiar with. It reflects first and foremost that our God is a God of relationship. Michael Lloyd, in *Café Theology* (Alpha 2005) reminds us that God 'is not only personal—he is also relational. There is relationship going on within the very being of God… a relationship that has eternally been going on between the Father, the Son and the Spirit.' Fatherhood, says Isaiah, that is everlasting.

Everlasting is a wonderful word. My earliest memory of it is happily derived from the joy of everlasting toffee! Yet, for some of us 'everlasting' will, by contrast, remind us of times when fathering literally 'ran out'. If our experience of fatherhood is filled with pain or empty with absence, the concept of an everlasting Father is challenging. But if we reach out to him we will discover that he has already reached out to us. His grace and tenderness will be in that embrace and fill us with eternal hope that doesn't depend on the past. Perhaps *eternal* Father may be a more helpful translation—a Father forever. My favourite, however, is that of Rob Lacey, whose *Word on the Street* (Zondervan 2005) paraphrase reads, 'the Father who stays'. Stay implies comfort, presence and security. So here, by way of introduction, is our Father God. The everlasting Father, the eternal parent, 'the Father who stays'.

....

Wonderful Counsellor, Mighty God, give me a fresh, liberating appreciation of what it means to be your precious child and to call you Father.

Discover something more of the Father's tender care in Isaiah 40:9–11.

WB

Undeserved adoption rights

Yet to all who received him, to those who believed in his name, he gave the right to become children of God.

Our local paper recently carried the story of a couple who have fostered over 40 children. Some years ago, they adopted one little boy who had particularly touched their hearts. When, two years later, his Mum gave birth to another little lad, they joyfully adopted him too. The boys are now aged three and five and have just been christened. Instead of the usual cake and crowd at home, a historic fort that the boys particularly enjoy was hired for a party. The accompanying photograph showed a happy family wreathed in smiles.

Visiting the Roman Baths in Bath I was reminded that such loving adoption is nothing new. The moving inscription on a surviving tombstone shared the memory, all these years later, of a baby girl who had lived just one year and nine months. Born into slavery, she had been adopted by an eminent Roman family who had obviously loved her dearly and were heartbroken at their loss.

The Romans accepted the spirit of adoption wholeheartedly, giving adopted sons and daughters the same rights and privileges—and obviously in this case, love—as their own children. God does just the same with us. We are born into 'slavery', but adopted as sons and daughters with equal rights and privileges, and he loves us dearly.

We hear a lot about rights. More than anything we seem to use them to weakly justify our position or the privileges we think we deserve in life. But these verses talk about rights given to us by God, which are justified by mercy and faith.

Additionally, we might think that 'by rights' it should be we who are received by *him* not this way round—but that's the nature of grace. It's the wonderful undeserved favour of an adoptive father God: the kiss of the king for the lowliest child.

....

Thank you Father, that you lifted me from the lowliest place of a helpless child on to the lap of the King, into whose face I can gaze—by right.

Read Romans 8:14–17 to learn more about our privileges as adopted children.

WB

Heirs and grace

By faith in Christ you are in direct relationship with God… Among us you are all equal. That is, we are all in a common relationship with Jesus Christ. Also, since you are Christ's family, then you are Abraham's famous 'descendant', heirs according to covenant promises.

Yesterday we mentioned the relevance of adoption to the ongoing story of God's grace towards his children. That grace is offered to *all* who will receive him as Father. No one is more 'in' with God than anyone else. Yes, some may be chosen for more prominent roles, or be given special tasks which appear to have more kudos. But whether we are a platform speaker or a platform cleaner, we each have equal status.

There is no favouritism in God's family. Sibling rivalry, so apparent in our earthly families, should never be an issue in relation to Father God. We all have equal value with equal inheritance.

Abraham was promised that he would be the father of a great nation: 'God's particular association with Abraham, Isaac and Jacob, the fathers of the nations of Israel, highlights his faithfulness in fulfilling the promises made to them. He… establishes a covenant with his people for their everlasting blessing' (*The Thematic Bible*, Hodder & Stoughton, 1996, p. 1360). Paul, who wrote this letter to the Galatians, tells us that we are made secure by another faithful promise of a very special kind of inheritance. As children of God we are promised everlasting life from and with an everlasting Father resulting in everlasting blessing.

Our son Benjamin often jokes about his 'inheritance'. As a descendant of his (imagined) fabulously wealthy parents, he lightheartedly tells us that he looks forward to a life of luxury and ease, living off his inheritance. We frequently tell him that, sadly, that fabulous inheritance will soon run out, as it will be needed to get him through university! Thankfully, he knows that there is one everlasting inheritance that he can depend on as an heir of a heavenly Father.

....

Father God, may the way I value those who share your inheritance with me reflect the value you place upon them as much-loved children.

Read Romans 2:25 to be reminded of the promise of a greater inheritance.

WB

Daddy cool

The resurrection life you received from God is… adventurously expec-
tant, greeting God with a child-like 'What's next, Papa?' God's Spirit
touches our spirits and confirms who we really are. We know who he
is, and we know who we are: Father and children. And we know we
are going to get what's coming to us—an unbelievable inheritance!

My Dad was the best. One of my joys as a young child was to wander
along the grassy footpath near our home just as I knew Dad would be
walking home from work. The path meandered for some distance, and
with each bend I would look ahead to try to spot him approaching
from the other direction. Finally, in the distance, I would see him and
shout out. He would look up, smile, and then squat, holding out his
arms so that I could run into them with shouts of 'Daddy! Daddy!'
Then he would lift me high on his shoulders to carry me home. Those
memories bring tears to my eyes, but they also offer a vivid image of
what my relationship with my Father God should be like.

It is still a joy to see a small child identify and run towards his
father. Once, while waiting in arrivals at Heathrow airport, I watched
as a little Jewish boy ran towards his Dad in a similar way with shouts
of 'Abba! Abba!': 'Daddy! Daddy!' to be embraced and lifted high, just
as I was, his face beaming with delight.

That sight and sound revived memories, but it also brought these
verses alive in a fresh way. That little boy knew exactly who his Daddy
was, even in the midst of the busy arrivals hall. Recognition led to relationship.

The Holy Spirit 'touches our hearts and confirms who we really
are'. Some of us without such memories may need the Holy Spirit to
help us understand who we 'really are' in relation to a tender Father
God. But all of us can run towards his open arms. Our recognition of
'Abba'—'Daddy' is the prelude to a relationship like no other.

....

Ask your Father God to help you recognize him as 'Abba'. Ask
another Christian to pray with you if you find that difficult to do.

                                                                                    WB

Just ask

'Do not be like them, for your Father knows what you need before you ask him. This, then, is how you should pray: "Our Father in heaven, hallowed is your name…"'

When a relationship is close, the one who knows us very well will often anticipate our needs. There is nothing like a 'nice cup of tea' offered thoughtfully just at the right moment! God also knows and anticipates our needs—for a whole lot more than a cup of tea. But we tend to get ourselves in a fix about these verses. 'If God knows what we need already' we say, 'why ask him?'

Imagine yourself as a child, wanting things you know your Father could provide and is happy to give. Would you just wait for those things and hope? No, you would ask. It's the natural thing for a child to do. A loving Father would want us to share our feelings with him so that he can respond to our needs. If we never have to ask for things we want we would soon take them, and him, for granted.

Asking is essential because it establishes our dependence on God. He doesn't want us to feel indebted to him, but to know that without him we can do nothing. He also delights in giving us what we need—and more. He may even sometimes withhold blessings he longs to give because we don't ask.

How often have you struggled on alone in a difficult situation only to have a friend say, 'Why on earth didn't you ask?' Well, God is saying, 'Why in heaven don't you ask?' How do we do that? These words of Jesus tell us: we must pray as children.

As Michael Lloyd says, prayer is 'like a child sitting and eating at the dinner table with the rest of the family and joining in its conversation' (*Café Theology*, pp. 268–9). Our Father sits alongside us with a listening ear. He longs to meet our needs.

....

Sit; ask. Your heavenly Father is listening and longs to hear you. Begin by praying the prayer that Jesus taught in these verses.

Read John 20:17 to be reminded who we share our Father with as 'family'.

WB

Faithful Father—rebellious children

You are our Father, though Abraham does not know us or Israel acknowledge us; you, O Lord, are our Father, our Redeemer from of old is your name.

Isaiah is praying prophetically to the Father of rebellious children. It is a heartfelt prayer both for his generation and those to come. The faithfulness of a Father has been rejected by his children. A precious relationship has been lost. He prays as a go-between remembering God's faithfulness, longing for relationship to be resumed. Barry Webb writes:

God's… deliverance of the Israelites from Egyptian bondage established a Father/child relationship between him and them, and through the whole experience he cherished them as his children. He felt their distress, saved them from the perils of the way, lifted them up and carried them when they were weak and rightly expected that they would return his love by being true to him. But sadly it was not so, they rebelled.
BIBLE SPEAKS TODAY: ISAIAH, IVP, 1996, PP. 241–2

Today's powerful Bible passage captures the pain of a parent in the face of rebellion and loss of relationship. But it also points to the heartbroken faithfulness of a Father God through generations, despite that rebellion and loss. God *did* turn his heart back to his children in response to Isaiah's plea, but not without voicing his fury and dismay at the estrangement and the discipline that would result.

These words are not easy reading, but they show us that God knows what it is to feel anger and distress at his children's rebellion—and to go on loving them, an experience that all parents will share to a greater or lesser degree. They also remind us that our relationship with God is not a weak and spineless dalliance between an overindulgent father and a spoilt child, but a relationship involving the full spectrum of parental experience from love and faithfulness to discipline and heartbreak.

....

Father God, don't let me take the heritage of my relationship with you lightly. Remind me of your faithfulness to me—but also of the debt I owe you as your child.

WB

Father of the fatherless

A father to the fatherless, a defender of widows, is God in his holy dwelling. God sets the lonely in families, he leads forth the prisoners with singing; but the rebellious live in a sun-scorched land.

I have seen these verses worked out practically so often that I never forget how much God cares for those without family. Orphans and widows are a vulnerable group to whom God shows special kindness. He expects his people to do the same. Consequently these verses are as much of a challenge to me as a Christian as they are a comfort to those who are fatherless or widowed.

It may seem an extreme notion for God to *defend* widows as he cares for them—but that he surely does! I have a friend who, as a widow herself, is involved in caring for and supporting young women in the early days following the loss of their partners. She can relay countless times when she has known or witnessed the certain protection of God, in incidents as wide-ranging as the changing of a car tyre on a busy road to her family's safety during a burglary. From the very beginning of her experience with all its pain and vulnerability, she took God at his word *from* his word, the Bible. He has fulfilled that word with protection, care and his special presence at her most desperate and heartbroken moments.

When we are without family, God can fill something of the empty space with himself. But the challenge of these verses extends wider than just our personal space. We live in a world dominated, often controversially, by the plight of the refugee, the displaced and the marginalized. Many are forced to leave wider family communities and closer family members to flee for their lives or their dignity. How do we respond, in the face of their experience, to God's call to defend the fatherless and set the lonely in families? How much does our action, or inaction, reflect the Father-heart of God?

....

Father, from the very depths of heaven you take the experience of the lonely to your heart. Help us to do the same on earth.

Read Deuteronomy 10:18 to see the extent to which God becomes a father to the fatherless.

WB

34

Daily provision

So do not worry, saying, 'What shall we eat?' or 'What shall we drink?' or 'What shall we wear?' For the pagans run after all these things, and your heavenly Father knows that you need them.

My children have helped me understand God's generous provision in a new way. I try hard not to spoil them, but if I do, they are at least old enough now to understand my motivation. Recently they took part in a seminar on parenting teenagers, answering the questions of hundreds of parents. (Yes—bribery was required!)

In response to a question my daughter explained that she did not expect me to provide more than her needs, but that the extras were a special expression of my love. Her recognition of that generous love does not depend on the extras but they gild it with a special patina.

God does that too! Several years ago, when money was tight, my husband encouraged me to use an unexpected £65 rebate to buy an evening dress for a special function. I had longed for a twenties-style beaded dress, but they were not so much in vogue then, and I was hesitant about using the money so frivolously. So I prayed that God would provide what I needed. Almost as soon as I got off the bus in town, I spotted a cream beaded dress in the window of a boutique. Knowing it was probably hundreds more than I could afford, I decided to ask, just in case… Imagine my amazement and delight when I was told that it was in the sale—at £65! God loves to spoil us too!

This provision of luxuries is all very well, but what about those who cannot meet their family's most basic needs? God will often choose to meet those needs through our response to the needy as we become channels of his compassion, self-sacrifice and provision. The poor are our responsibility. When he is so generous to us, how can we not be generous too?

....

Father, as you give good gifts to your children, help me to pass on those gifts in gratitude.

Read Matthew 7:9–11 and consider 'How much more…?'

WB

Delight and discipline

My son, do not despise the Lord's discipline and do not resent his rebuke, because the Lord disciplines those he loves, as parents the children they delight in.

Discipline is not without negative connotations. We are quick to visualize a strict Victorian schoolteacher or a joyless existence of more 'don'ts' than 'dos'. But discipline, worked out as intended, is an essential structure for security, whatever our age.

Occasionally I have watched one of those TV programmes in which a childcare expert visits a family whose discipline has gone awry. It always seems to me that the parents need discipline as much as the children! They struggle with maintaining control and have even begun to dislike their offspring as a result. Those children show signs of anger and insecurity and long for order. The expert arrives. Boundaries for behaviour are set and, often after a few hiccups, the children begin to enjoy their parents again as the parents delight in their children.

Those who have children of their own, who know them well or teach them, will have learnt that discipline does not work without delight. Neither does delight result without discipline. If discipline is missing—in children or adults—there won't be much to delight in. As our children grow older, they even begin to appreciate the benefits of discipline, a benefit that applies as much to an athlete or musician in practice as to a parent and child relationship.

God as Father does not flinch from discipline. He sets clear boundaries for our behaviour, our lifestyle and our Christian pathway that protect us and lead us to delight. If we persistently wander without remorse, he may choose to discipline us, to find a way to 'bring us up short' on our wandering pathway and point us—through discipline—back in the direction of delight. We must 'forget not all his benefits' (Psalm 103), even those of discipline.

....

Father, teach me, discipline me, draw me to yourself on your pathway of life, that I may be a delight to your heart.

Read Deuteronomy 8:5 for a model of discipline.

WB

Father of compassion

As a father has compassion on his children, so the Lord has compassion on those who fear him; for he knows how we were formed, he remembers that we are dust.

'The compassion of God,' says *The Thematic Bible* (Hodder & Stoughton, 1996) is like 'that of caring parents towards their children. Despite their sinfulness and rebellion against him, God shows kindness to his creatures' (p. 955).

Thank goodness that God as our Father has the measure of us. He knows how we are made and he doesn't expect perfection. That doesn't mean we can be lazy in our attitude towards following his way. But it does mean that he knows our human limitations and is there to help us live within—and sometimes beyond—them. It also means that he will show compassion when, despite our best efforts, we slip up.

If we show genuine remorse and regret at the damage we have done to our relationship with him in the process, he will show tenderness.

Parenting teenage girls is an interesting exercise! I fear that my daughter is much like me at her age, so I do at least understand something of where she is coming from. Her father, however, is at a complete loss, despite the fact that some of her 'interesting' traits are down to him as well as me. He doesn't as much forget *how* she was made, but he does forget what she is made of; that she is a genetic combination of both of us. That genetic combination causes its fair share of rebellion.

Despite her rebellion, we do have compassion on her—when we can be gracious enough! In the midst of setting boundaries we forgive her simply because we know that like us she is only human—and a teenage human at that.

God also knows that we are human. If we do our best to honour the boundaries he sets and genuinely ask for forgiveness when we cross them—he will have compassion on us.

....

Your compassion, with its many facets, shines like a jewel. Help me reflect its light in the darkest places, Lord.

Read 2 Corinthians 1:3 to discover how we might pass on another facet of that compassion first shown to us.

WB

Waiting for the prodigal

'When he was still a long way off, his father saw him. His heart pounding, he ran out, embraced him and kissed him.'

The father had undoubtedly been looking out for his son because he saw him from 'a long way off'. Perhaps he walked to the edge of his estate every evening after supper hoping to see the familiar figure of the wayward boy he loved so much. Certainly he would have imagined the nightmare scenarios that might be befalling his son. Maybe he turned from those all too vivid pictures with a fearful heart and longed for the moment of reconciliation in the sleepless hours of the night. Perhaps he had imagined that moment in such detail that even when his son appeared at last, weight lost, clothes ragged, body battered, head dropped in dejection, he recognized him and ran to embrace him.

God recognizes us as his children despite the battering of sin and the raggedness of selfish waywardness. He looks out for us and aches for us long before we take the decision to return to him.

We learn as much about the Father heart of God from what the father in this parable didn't do as from what he did do. There was no reprimand for the son in wanting his inheritance early, no chasing after him to demand apology, no lecture or 'I told you so' thinly veiled on return. The father gave his son space for independent choice—even if it meant mistakes and danger; time for him to spend following his own way before recognizing the need for repentance; and love from a heart bursting with compassion in the welcome home.

The grace and love of our Father asks that we look out for and welcome the prodigals in our lives, whoever and wherever they are. And that we treat each other with the same grace, love and compassion that the waiting father first showed us.

....

Father God, I know what it is to be held in your forgiving arms. Help me to spread my arms wide to others with that same grace, mercy and love.

Read Matthew 5:23–24 to learn about our need to be reconciled with each other.

WB

Lavished love

How great is the love the Father has lavished on us, that we should be called children of God! And that is what we are!

At the beginning of our time together I shared something of how I 'spoil' my children. I love doing it—and I have a feeling that they don't mind too much either! Well, here are God's own spoiling verses for us, his children. If 'lavish' isn't a word to be connected to extravagant, OTT love, what is? It's a love illustrated, as we learnt earlier, by our adoption as sons and daughters of God. But the Father's love isn't just about being spoilt with the extras. It needs foundations. We all know children who are spoilt by material extras, but woefully lacking in the security and confidence that the foundations of parental love should give.

God's parenting gives us a model for those foundations, but it also reminds us of what we can be confident of in our relationship with him.

Michael Youssef in *The Prayer that God Answers* (Nelson, 2000, pp. 29–30) tells us that the Father's love provides four things. First, *freedom from fear*, because we know that he loves us and that everything that happens to us—whether we understand it or not—will ultimately turn out for good (Romans 8:28). Second, *confidence*, because we have the hope of heaven and the joy that brings. We know we will be with our Father when this life is through (John 14:2). Third, *companionship*, because our heavenly Father is never too busy to spend time with us. In fact he longs for our company, even delights in it (Psalm 21:6)! And finally, *provision*, because he tells us that he will provide for all our needs according to his riches (Philippians 4:19).

That's just the foundation of the extravagant, unstoppable love of God. What we build *upon* it and *with* it in our lives, and how we enlarge our 'plot' by drawing others into God's love, is very much down to us.

....

Father God—as you lavish your love on me, help me to lavish that same love on others.

Read 1 Corinthians 13:4–8a for a description of true love.

WB

Suffering child… suffering Father

Going a little farther, he fell with his face to the ground and prayed, 'My Father, if this is possible, may this cup be taken from me. Yet not as I will, but as you will'… He went away a second time and prayed, 'My Father, if it is not possible for this cup to be taken away unless I drink it, may your will be done.'

Here, Jesus uses the word *Abba*—Daddy, the intimate address we referred to previously. His words reveal a painful struggle, but they also illustrate the relationship of a Father and Son whose hearts are one; intent on doing what they know must be done while regretting the path of pain that must be followed in order to achieve the greater good.

In Mel Gibson's film *The Passion of the Christ* a large tear falls from heaven as Jesus suffers crucifixion. At first I thought this apparently melodramatic Hollywood pun unnecessary. Then I realized that Mel Gibson knew that he would have to find a way to communicate his belief that God the Father was not an indifferent spectator of his Son's suffering—or that of any of his children—but an agonized one.

Not everyone agrees that God the Father shares our suffering. But those who have known the tender love of God in the midst of it would surely agree. These verses became very real to me just a few weeks ago. They prepared me for the diagnosis of the second cancer—totally unrelated to the first—that I have faced within six years. I had read these verses during my own Gethsemane the first time around. But I now recognized that God weeps *with* me in that garden of suffering.

Suffering *outside* the context of relationship has no meaning. *In* relationship it knows compassion, tenderness, love, companionship and dependency. In my case it knows the compassion, tenderness, love and companionship of my heavenly Father who has set the foundations of extravagant love in my life. God never leaves us alone in the darkness, even if we can't yet see him. He *will* emerge, bright from the gloom.

'Abba', I whisper in my darkness. 'Daddy—I will trust you.'

Read Luke 23:34 to see how Jesus' relationship with 'Abba' enabled him to look beyond his own pain to the needs of others.

WB

In my Father's house

'In my Father's house are many rooms; if it were not so, I would have told you. I am going there to prepare a place for you.'

I have something of an obsession with homestyle magazines—those glossy monthlies often found in the dentist's waiting room or the hairdresser's chair, which transport us to the world of permanently vacuumed carpets, matching bed-linen and smear-free kitchen work-tops. I'm just as bad about home-search and home-building TV programmes. Not for me the fluffy artificial impermanence of mere decorating. I'm not interested in cheap and temporary domestic cosmetics. It's the *home* and all it means for security and family life as well as design, function, colour and light that matters to me.

I don't think my desire for a beautiful welcoming home is a materialistic one. I think it reflects a spiritual longing: a search for the home that really will be perfect and permanent in every way—heaven. I think we all have a heavenly homing device; something deep within us that is calling us home to the Father.

In these verses Jesus' use of the word 'heaven' literally means 'dwelling places', implying permanence and security.

Of course, heaven is more about the presence of God than the environment, and more about what it won't contain than what it will: no more pain or suffering, no more loss or tears, no more temptation or regret, no schedules, rushing, deadlines and disillusionment. No more darkness or death. We can hardly begin to imagine it.

Jesus gets us started by telling us that our Father's house has many rooms and that he has gone ahead to prepare a place for us, exactly to the design specification that he knows will suit us best. We're going home—and what a wonderful welcome there will be! God, the eternal 'Father who stays' who has loved, guided, redeemed and cherished will meet with us, settle us in, and we will stay with him—for ever.

....

Father God, fill me with an anticipation of heaven and a love for your Son inspired by your Holy Spirit, so that I may find my way safely home.

Read Revelation 21:1—22:5 for a vision of heaven.

WB

How do you know God? Is he a distance task-master or a loving Father? Does your Christian life read like a rule-book or a love story? Living life by a set of rules can seem simpler, I think that's why I like to-do lists—especially at busy times. But a to-do list including 'kiss my husband', 'give Mum a hug', 'help a pensioner today' would indicate a very sad, superficial life with no real depth to relationships. Real relationships are not lived by rules and to-do lists, they flow out of a loving heart.

God wants heart-to-heart relationships with us. We can expect to hear him call to us—like he called to Adam and Eve in the garden in the cool of the evening. He wanted to walk with them and he wants to walk with us—talking over our concerns and joys in unhurried conversations; conversations without an agenda or a list. Don't miss the opportunities he gives you to get to know him better.

Sometimes we need to make that unhurried time possible. Jesus took time out to be with his disciples, listening to them explain what they'd been doing. Jesus still wants to take time out with us—his twenty-first-century disciples. Accept the invitation he gives you to spend time with him, but also expect close encounters with him throughout your day.

Sometimes you will find God speaking through the daily routine: cooking, gardening, travelling. Expect to hear him in times of crisis, but also expect silent times when you learn to rely on the knowledge of God gained in those heart-to-heart times. New relationships need constant contact—almost a perpetual honeymoon. More mature relationships can survive and deepen in silence or through temporary distance.

Make this hymn a prayer, inviting God to lead you into a deeper relationship with himself. Don't miss the opportunities he gives.

Drop Thy still dews of quietness,
Till all our strivings cease;
Take from our souls the strain and stress,
And let our ordered lives confess
The beauty of Thy peace.
JOHN GREENLEAF WHITTIER (1807–92)

The road to Damascus

Saul began to destroy the church. Going from house to house, he dragged off both men and women and put them in prison. Those who had been scattered preached the word wherever they went.

Paul, or Saul as he was called in the beginning, was proud that he was a Jew and a Roman citizen, proud of his training in the Old Testament law, proud that he was a member of the Pharisees in Jerusalem. He was horrified that some Jews were betraying God, worshipping Jesus of Nazareth as the Messiah and saying he had risen from the dead. He was given official permission to break up the fellowships in Jerusalem, imprisoning the leaders. Determined to stamp out this new faith, he was sent to Damascus to break up the churches there.

Paul didn't know that God had already chosen him to be his messenger to take the wonderful news of the crucified and risen Jesus to the ends of the earth. Nor did he realize that the persecution he had begun was not destroying the church, but spreading it and increasing the numbers of believers, as the Christians of Jerusalem fled to other cities.

These small groups of believers must have wondered how they would survive when they faced persecution. We too can easily lose faith in God's power to protect and build his church and to change people's lives. I have prayed for several people to become Christians over the years and I do lose heart. I begin to think that it is just impossible for God to change them. Not because they are angry, violent people, like Paul, but simply because they seem blind to the claims of God on their lives. But God can change the proudest and most determined unbelievers. And he *will* build his church. Growth may seem slow here in Britain, but there are many parts of the world where the church is growing by leaps and bounds—where all kinds of people are being transformed by the power of God.

....

Lord, as I pray for those I know who do not follow you, give me faith that you can change anyone and build your church.

Read 1 Peter 2:4–10 to discover the building materials God uses.

MK

A life transformed

'"Saul, Saul, why do you persecute me? It is hard for you to kick against the goads." Then I asked, "Who are you, Lord?" "I am Jesus, whom you are persecuting," the Lord replied. "Now get up and stand on your feet."'

Our reading from Acts comes near the end of Paul's very active life of travel, preaching and building churches. He was a chained prisoner, on trial, defending himself before King Agrippa, and telling his story before being sent to Rome where, as far as we know, he was eventually executed.

Paul told King Agrippa that, on the road to Damascus, he had fallen down before the living Lord, blinded by a light brighter than the sun; that he had obeyed Jesus and got on with the job Jesus gave him. He had travelled all over the Roman and Greek world telling everyone, Jew and Gentile, to turn from darkness to light, from the power of Satan to God, preaching about God's grace and forgiveness through the cross of Christ.

God had laid hold of him. All his learning and all his abilities would now be used to serve God's purposes. He was a changed man—his attitudes, his behaviour, his beliefs about God and about himself were all transformed by the love of God. Many years ago I read *The Cross and the Switchblade*, which told the story of gang leaders in New York becoming Christians and having their whole lives turned round. More recently I have read of men of violence in Northern Ireland meeting Jesus and becoming passionate preachers of a gospel of love and peace.

For most of us, becoming a Christian is not quite so dramatic and the change in us is not immediately so noticeable. Nor are many of us told to give up all we have and go to the ends of the earth. But dramatically or quietly, when we turn to Jesus we have a new purpose and we begin a process of transformation that lasts a lifetime.

....

In what ways has your life been transformed since you first became a disciple of Jesus?

Read Galatians 1:11–24 for another account by Paul of how he became an apostle.

MK

Time to think

[Paul] talked and debated with the Grecian Jews, but they tried to kill him. When the believers learned of this, they took him down to Caesarea and sent him off to Tarsus.

When Paul arrived in Damascus, a Christian called Ananias cared for him and baptized him. Filled with the Holy Spirit, Paul at once began to teach about Jesus, upsetting the enemies of the church who thought he was on their side. They plotted to kill him and he escaped from Damascus down the city walls in a basket! In Jerusalem Barnabas introduced him to the church, but again this was too much for many of the Jews. Hurriedly he was put on a ship and sent back to his birthplace, Tarsus.

It was some time, perhaps as long as ten years, before we hear of him again. I expect Paul hadn't planned on these years out of the action. He knew what God wanted him to do and he started straight-away preaching in Damascus and then in Jerusalem. Maybe these years were necessary for him to think through what it meant to be a disciple of Jesus. He probably spent time with the Old Testament, seeing how it pointed forward to Jesus. He was always a busy, active man and he needed time to think and pray and to learn about himself and about his new Lord.

Some people are good at stopping, letting all the everyday things drop away to spend time with God, but many of us are not. Paul needed time to think and pray, and so do we. The Lord's transforming power doesn't work like a fairy godmother's wand. God changes us just so far as we are willing to be changed. So we need time when we can look at our own lives, our relationships and our attitudes, talk them over in prayer before the Lord and let him teach us his ways. We need time to read the Bible and begin to understand what God is saying to us as we read.

....

How often do you spend quality time with the Lord? To serve him well in the busyness of life, we all need times of quiet worship.

Read Acts 13:16–41 to see Paul using the Old Testament to back up his preaching about Jesus.

MK

Enemies transformed

After they had been severely flogged, they were thrown into prison, and the jailer... put them in the inner cell and fastened their feet in the stocks. About midnight Paul and Silas were praying and singing hymns to God, and the other prisoners were listening to them. Suddenly...

Paul knew about prisons and floggings. Stoning, beatings and imprisonment had happened to him in a number of the towns and cities of the Roman empire. Disturbing the peace was a serious offence and local officials were angry when Paul arrived and created a stir. But Paul also knew about prisons because he had been responsible for imprisoning Christians. As we read what happened between Paul and the jailer, we see two lives transformed by Jesus.

Suddenly an earthquake destroyed the prison. The jailer, who thought all his prisoners had escaped, was about to kill himself, but Paul stopped him, reassuring him that they were all still there. The jailer, overwhelmed by this thoughtfulness, gave his life to Jesus Christ, cleaned them up and fed them. After encouraging the new fellowship in Philippi, Paul and Silas went on their way.

Paul had written in his letter to the Romans, 'Do not repay anyone evil for evil. Bless those who persecute you.' So he made sure that the prisoners and the jailer were safe: Paul had been transformed. He told the jailer of the wonderful grace of God—and another life was transformed.

Would we have escaped as fast as we could and not cared what happened to the jailer? 'If your enemies are hungry, feed them,' Paul wrote (Romans 12:20). How do we handle family disputes and quarrels with neighbours? How do we react to meanness and gossip? Do we fight back, or walk away? Or do we care enough to try and turn the situation round? The way we handle enmity and injury from others has the power to transform their lives and ours.

....

Pray that the Lord will show you any hostile and angry relationships that could be transformed by love—and food!

Read Romans 12:9–21, about how to treat enemies.

MK

Transformed from the inside out!

Therefore, I urge you, brothers and sisters, in view of God's mercy, to offer your bodies as living sacrifices, holy and pleasing to God— this is your spiritual act of worship. Do not conform... to the pattern of this world, but be transformed by the renewing of your mind.

Not many of us are completely content with the way we are. Our character, our relationships, our job and our home could all do with a little adjustment. Most of us would like to be more attractive, slimmer perhaps, different in one way or another. We would like to conform to this world's idea of attractiveness. This may be why there are so many television programmes about makeovers. Gardens and houses are given expert treatment and transformed with stunning new decor. And people too are transformed: hair, face, body shape and clothes are given a new lease of life with cosmetics, plastic surgery and dieting.

These external transformations *can* make a difference, because having confidence in what we look like helps in our everyday dealings with other people. But deep-down change on the inside is far harder to find. Paul was changed when Jesus met him on the road to Damascus. That is where inner transformation began for him, and when we turn to the Lord in repentance and faith this remarkable process of transformation begins in us. This process takes a lifetime and eventually brings us to full Christian maturity.

Paul says, 'Be transformed, by the renewing of your mind'. God does not make us into transformed people while we sit and do nothing. It is our life's greatest adventure to *walk* with God through thick and thin and *work* with God as he transforms us in body, mind and soul. This involves all the Christian disciplines: praying, reading our Bibles, and being in fellowship groups where we help each other grow. It involves a lifetime of his transforming grace as we develop well-formed maturity.

Lord, there are things I don't like about myself. Help me to open up my heart and life to you so that you can begin to change me on the inside.

All followers of Jesus can look forward to instant transformation. Read 1 Corinthians 15:50–57 to find out more.

MK

Transformed into his likeness

And we, who with unveiled faces all reflect the Lord's glory, are being transformed into his likeness with ever-increasing glory, which comes from the Lord, who is the Spirit.

Paul's vision of Jesus on the road to Damascus was filled with a light brighter than the sun. The disciples, Peter, James and John, once went with Jesus up a mountain and saw him transfigured: his face shone like the sun and his clothes became as white as the light. The disciples were terrified for they were seeing Jesus full of the glory of heaven. Paul realized that he too, like Peter and the others, had seen Jesus transformed by the blinding light of heaven's glory. He told the Corinthian Christians that they, together with all believers down the ages, would be transformed, transfigured, shining like the sun, in the heaven God has prepared for his people.

But even today, as we read these notes, this heavenly brightness and beauty is gradually growing within us, our lives becoming more beautiful as God transforms us. And this transformation has a purpose—to change us into the likeness of Jesus.

Jesus, the Son of God, who sits at the right hand of the Father in all the glory of heaven, walked for 30 years in our world, knowing all its pains and joys. When we read the story of Jesus we find out what he was like, but we also learn what *we* should be like. We see his love and compassion, taking time to listen, loving the unloved and the outcasts, taking the role of a servant, sacrificing himself for others. We see him facing suffering, not answering back, forgiving and healing. One day we shall be like him and see him as he is in glory. Meanwhile God is transforming us, in our ordinary everyday lives and in all our ordinary relationships. Our task is to learn from him and to be willing to be changed into his likeness.

....

Lord, help me today to see that you are transforming me. May I be more like Jesus in all I think and say and do.

Read Matthew 17:1–15. Notice how everyone had to come down from the mountain to the everyday problems of life.

MK

The transformed personality

But the fruit of the Spirit is love, joy, peace, patience, kindness, goodness, faithfulness, gentleness and self-control.

What does the transformed life look like? In Paul's letter to the church in Galatia, there are two lists. The first contains what Paul calls the acts of the sinful nature. It includes drunkenness and sexual immorality, part of his world as they are of ours. We can see them and their effects in the media as well as in lives around us. These may not be our weaknesses, but discord, jealousy, selfish ambition and envy touch all of us at times.

Paul's second list includes a range of qualities that are the fruit of the Holy Spirit's transforming work in our lives. These are the marks of someone who is becoming like Jesus; they demonstrate the character of God. When we read the story of Paul's life we can see how anger, hatred, discord and ruthless ambition were transformed into love, patience and self-control.

Sometimes our feelings and emotions betray us; we may *feel* jealous inside, for example, but if we fight the feeling and don't *act* jealously then we have begun to change. For me, there are people I can't love, but I ask the Lord to help me act as though I do. There are moments when I am very impatient and irritated, but I try to act patiently. And as I exercise self-control over my natural desire to show my irritation and impatience, then I sense that the very process is changing and transforming me. I have heard people excuse anger and selfishness by saying that they can't help it, they are made that way. It is hard to fight our own nature. But the Lord promises us his transforming power, and if we really want to be changed, then we find, as we look back, that the miracle has happened and grace has been at work in our weaknesses.

....

Pray over these qualities. Take them one by one, and ask the Lord to show you where you may need to exercise each one in your relationships, at work, in your fellowship and in your own heart.

MK

Transformed friendships

Tychicus will tell you all the news about me. He is a dear brother, a faithful minister and fellow-servant in the Lord. I am sending him to you for the express purpose that you may know about our circumstances and that he may encourage your hearts.

Paul had friends—friends he worked with, friends he stayed with, friends he travelled with. This passage comes at the end of his letter from prison to the Christians in the town of Colossae. Paul ended many of his letters with greetings to and from friends—the letter to Rome lists 35 people! When he became a Christian, Paul needed friendly help. In Damascus he needed Ananias to introduce him to the local fellowship. It cannot have been easy for those Christians to accept him when he had ill-treated people they knew and loved. Later, when he went back to Jerusalem, it must have been just as hard for the disciples there. That time Barnabas helped him to overcome their suspicion. Paul travelled all over what is now Turkey, Lebanon and Syria, Greece and Italy, and he travelled with a number of companions. Barnabas was one of them.

The other day I went to a school reunion. I met women I had not seen for over 40 years. Most of the working and parenting part of our lives had happened between the day we left school and this sunny afternoon in the school hall. I realized that there were one or two there who could have been my close friends over the years, but we simply had not kept in touch. Friends have dropped out of my world steadily over the years. Yet we need friends—those who are not just neighbours, or fellow church members, or relatives, or work colleagues, although all of those can be friends as well. We need a few close friends whom we can trust, whose company we enjoy and with whom we can share every part of our lives. Transformed friendship helps us build transformed lives, as we pray, share, encourage and sometimes admonish each other.

....

Lord, help me to value friendship and to devote time and love to keeping my friends. Help us to help each other grow into maturity in Christ.

Read Paul's short letter to Philemon, about a runaway slave. This is friendship at work.

MK

A transformed community

Love must be sincere. Hate what is evil; cling to what is good. Be devoted to one another with mutual affection. Honour one another above yourselves… Share with God's people who are in need. Practise hospitality.

Our Christian transformation is not a private affair. Much of the transforming change in our lives comes from rubbing up against others in fellowship together. Paul describes the local fellowship of believers as a body with different parts; like the arms and legs of our physical bodies, we cannot live or work separately from the body of Christ, the church. Again and again he tells us to be devoted to one another, to serve one another, to carry one another's burdens, to forgive each other, to encourage one another, to look to the interests of one another.

Today many people live very lonely lives, moving house, changing jobs, and losing touch with people, even with family. Nearly a third of all households in the UK consist of someone living on their own. We need community and in some places the church is the only community on offer. But when we look at our own fellowship, what do we see? Is there open love for anyone who comes in? Are we willing to be involved in each other's lives? When the lonely or the handicapped come, are they welcomed? Are there any kinds of people who would feel out of place? Is there loving service into the community?

There are one or two jobs I am asked to do in my church that I really enjoy. But the other day I discovered I had signed my name up to help with a children's holiday club. I had forgotten completely that I had done so. My heart sank when I got the letter telling me all about it. Yet in spite of the hard physical work, I know that in the process of working together over a week, praying and caring for each other and the children, I will learn what it means to be the transformed, loving people of God.

....

Lord, show me how I can love and transform my fellowship and the people in it. And help me to allow my fellowship with them to transform me.

Read 1 Corinthians 12:12–28 for another description by Paul of the Church as a body.

MK

A world-transforming church

Since I have been longing for many years to see you, I plan to do so when I go to Spain. I hope to visit you while passing through and to have you assist me on my journey there.

All round the world, every Sunday, people are praying, 'Your kingdom come.' The transforming power of Jesus is not just for our own lives, nor just for our fellowships, but for the whole world. Christians are called to do what they can to make the world a better place, and God's amazing plan is to use his church to change his world. So in supporting churches all round the world, we are helping to spread his kingdom.

Paul linked churches together as he travelled. He went on foot over hundreds of miles—it was hard work and took time. He wrote letters and these had to be carried by messengers on foot, and shared by churches in neighbouring towns. He helped the fellowships to be aware of each other's needs and when one was having a hard time, another church would send gifts for the relief of the poor. In our reading he was taking money from Greece to Jerusalem.

So how do we take our part in the transformation of our world through large and small Christian communities? We may support those who plant churches—Paul was asking the Roman church to support his travels to Spain. We may find out what is happening to Christians in other places by reading up about them—as these churches did in Paul's letters. We may give money as the Macedonian churches had done. And we may be involved in informed prayer for our fellow Christians at home and abroad.

I have just read a letter about the Christian church in Turkey, where there is tension between Muslims and Christians. I now need to make sure that I act on what I have read by praying and sharing this news. This is one small way I can help the Christians of Turkey and help his kingdom come.

....

With so many needs around the world, you need God to show you the part he wants you to play. Ask for his help.

MK

Women transformed

You are all [children] of God through faith in Christ Jesus, for all of you who were baptized into Christ have clothed yourselves with Christ. There is neither Jew nor Greek, slave nor free, male nor female, for you are all one in Christ Jesus.

My grandmother was widowed at the age of 40 with five children. She lost her home; she had no pension and no job. She was an educated woman, but she couldn't vote, couldn't get a degree, couldn't study medicine or law, all because she was a woman.

When Paul arrived in a town, he usually went to the synagogue to tell the Jewish community about Jesus. When he arrived in Philippi it seemed that there wasn't a synagogue, only a group of women who prayed outside the town beside a river. A woman named Lydia came to faith in Jesus, was baptized and took Paul and Silas home with her, and the new group of believers met in her house.

Even today many of us are accustomed to male-led churches, so we may be surprised to find a woman hosting and leading this new fellowship. Paul included many women among his friends and fellow workers in the churches. As well as Lydia, there was Phoebe, a deacon, and Priscilla who, with her husband, taught in the church that met in her house. Paul encouraged husbands to love their wives and to honour them, just as he told slave masters to care for and honour their slaves. I expect some men had to change radically when they came to faith.

We may feel that being a woman is still a bit of a handicap, in our workplaces, and in the church. How should we react? Not stridently, demanding our own rights, but by supporting other women, encouraging them and sometimes suggesting to the leadership that their gifts should be used. The Spirit's transforming power changed the church so that old inequalities disappeared and men and women, slaves and free, could worship together, and go out and begin to change the world.

....

Pray for women you know who juggle home, family and work— and want to serve the Lord in the church. Is there a friend you can encourage and support?

Read Luke 10:38–42. The kitchen is not always the best place to be!

MK

Transformed by love

Love is patient, love is kind. It does not envy, it does not boast, it is not proud. It is not rude, it is not self-seeking, it is not easily angered, it keeps no record of wrongs.

Growing more like Jesus means growing in love. Paul spells out what love really means in this chapter, one that is often read at weddings. Even unbelievers respond to these wonderful words, knowing that if only people were like this the world would be transformed. But Paul knew that this love comes out of the relationship of the Father, Son and Holy Spirit and that it is only as the Holy Spirit works in us to transform us into the likeness of Jesus, do we begin to show this kind of love in our lives.

Love isn't something that we feel, that comes and goes, so that we were kind yesterday but don't feel like it today, 'It *always* protects, *always* trusts, *always* hopes, *always* perseveres'. It means being patient even when we are irritated and don't feel loving. It means being kind, even to someone who is being unkind. It means never bringing up the things other people have done that have hurt you—never scoring points.

There are many different kinds of emotions that we call love. Sometimes 'love' can betray us and spoil our own and other people's lives—an obsessive love that never lets go of a son; a sentimental love that won't discipline a child properly; a jealous possessive love that won't share a friend; an overwhelming sexual love that breaks up marriage and family. Perhaps some of us have learnt what love is like when we have children. When we *have* to get up in the night, every night. When we have to watch them leave home and make mistakes. When we wait for a wayward teenager to come home. Then we understand a little of the way our Father loves us. In humility and gratitude we can only try to love others in the same way.

••

Lord, teach me how to love; stop me when I begin to speak or act without love. Help me to love you by loving those around me.

Try learning 1 Corinthians 13 by heart.

MK

Transformed by prayer

I pray that out of his glorious riches he may strengthen you with power through his Spirit in your inner being, so that Christ may dwell in your hearts through faith... that you, being rooted and established in love, may have the power, together with all the saints, to grasp how wide and long and high and deep is the love of Christ... that you may be filled to the measure of all the fullness of God.

Have you ever felt overwhelmed by joyous, passionate emotion? Paul's letter to the Ephesians, probably written from prison, is amazingly breathless, with hardly any full stops. Perhaps he had been isolated for a time and then someone was available to take down his words so that they poured out in a great outburst of praise and prayer. He longed to tell the churches he had planted how much he loved them and prayed for them.

Paul wants his readers to know the spiritual resources that are theirs in Christ. He tells them *that* he is praying for them and tells them *what* he is praying for them. We may know with our heads that the Spirit can strengthen us with all the power of his glorious riches, but how do we practise the reality of that strengthening power in our daily lives? Kneeling before the Lord (for we need a physical as well as a mental attitude of prayer sometimes), we bring every aspect of our lives to his transforming power and love. Then we pray for others in the same way.

Prayer is transformation—it increases our love for those we pray for because we are longing for them to become what God wants them to be. Prayer is transformation—unbelievably and miraculously it is the way God chooses to work. He achieves his purposes in our lives through our prayers: 'He is able to do immeasurably more than all we ask or imagine.' Paul may have been in prison with no way to contact the people he cared for, but he had plenty of time for passionate, active, effective prayer.

....

When we think we can do nothing for someone we love, then we need to know that through prayer we can bring the Lord's transforming power and love into their lives.

MK

Looking back on a transformed life

I am already being poured out like a drink offering, and the time has come for my departure. I have fought the good fight, I have finished the race, I have kept the faith. Now there is in store for me the crown of righteousness.

This is probably the last letter that Paul wrote. He is in prison and senses that he has not long to live. He ends the letter with some very moving messages. He is looking back and assessing his life's work. He is no longer the proud young man he once was, but he knows that he has achieved great things for God. He has planted churches across the whole of the known world. Maybe missionaries from Spain were already travelling to the distant islands of Britain. As he awaits death, he knows that the Lord will bring him safely through to heaven, fully and totally transformed.

Paul had an overwhelming passion for Jesus and he understood that the cross where Jesus died was the powerful centre of the grace, mercy and love of God. He wrote, 'We preach Christ crucified: a stumbling block to Jews and foolishness to Gentiles, but to those whom God has called, both Jews and Greeks, Christ the power of God and the wisdom of God' (1 Corinthians 1:23–24). The Lord who loved him and was willing to die for him had totally captured his heart and life. Transformed by this love affair with Jesus, he fought a good fight and finished the race.

> *Were the whole realm of nature mine,*
> *That were an offering far too small;*
> *Love so amazing, so divine,*
> *Demands my life, my soul, my all!*
> ISAAC WATTS (1674–1748)

....

Isaac Watts wrote these words in 1707. Join with him and with Paul in worshipping the Lord, whose love has transformed us and who calls us to give him our all.

MK

What prompted you to respond to God? Paul was confronted by Jesus, the one whose followers he'd persecuted. Paul had been zealous as a persecutor. Now he became zealous as a follower of Christ—even when that meant a prison sentence.

Today people still respond to dramatic encounters with Jesus, though many of us get to know him in gentler ways. Take time to reflect on how you first came to know Jesus. What difference has he made in your life? Are you still walking close to him? Do you spend time talking to him, expecting to hear him talking to you? Do you let him touch your heart and emotions as well as your mind and actions? How does your love relationship with him affect others?

Your relationship with God is not meant to be exclusive and isolating. As Margaret Killingray mentioned, we are part of a world-transforming church.

When Paul tried to explain to the Corinthians what church was supposed to be like, he used the human body as an illustration: 'The way God designed our bodies is a model for understanding our lives together as a church: every part dependent on every other part, the parts we mention and the parts we don't, the parts we see and the parts we don't. If one part hurts, every other part is involved in the hurt, and in the healing. If one part flourishes, every other part enters into the exuberance' (1 Corinthians 12:25–26, *The Message*).

This body has many parts: 'A body isn't just a single part blown up into something huge. It's all the different-but-similar parts arranged and functioning together. If Foot said, "I'm not elegant like Hand, embellished with rings; I guess I don't belong to this body," would that make it so? If Ear said, "I'm not beautiful like Eye, limpid and expressive; I don't deserve a place on the head," would you want to remove it from the body? If the body was all eye, how could it hear? If all ear, how could it smell? As it is, we see that God has carefully placed each part of the body right where he wanted it' (1 Corinthians 12:14–18, *The Message*).

Let the body-picture Paul paints affect your thinking over the next two weeks as Wendy Virgo focuses on how we know God together, rather than as individuals.

All together

They devoted themselves to the apostles' teaching, and to fellowship, to the breaking of bread and to prayer. Everyone was filled with awe and many signs and wonders were done by the apostles. All the believers were together...

It was a new day: not even the new believers fully realized the extent of its newness! They were among the crowd that had come up to Jerusalem for Pentecost, had heard a commotion and, running into the temple square, had been transfixed to hear a dozen or so uncouth-looking men shouting about God in many different languages! Then one of those men had climbed on a wall and explained fluently what was happening.

He had declared that an Old Testament prophecy was being fulfilled before them: God was pouring out his Spirit! He further proclaimed that Jesus of Nazareth, who had recently been crucified, was in fact the Son of God, and had risen from death. Seated at the right hand of God the Father, he had now sent forth the Holy Spirit.

Instead of jeering and dismissing this preaching, the people became afraid. If this were true, they were guilty of murdering the Messiah! 'What shall we do?' they shouted. 'Repent of your sins, be baptized, and receive the Holy Spirit!' came the reply. Three thousand responded. They knew then what Jesus had meant about being born again. They felt clean, forgiven, like starting all over again. But as they talked together, it was like rediscovering one another: they had all changed. They found they wanted to be together, to learn, to exchange new perspectives, and yes, simply because they loved each other. Suddenly, it felt like family.

Together they listened daily to the apostles' teachings; together they learned to pray; together they expressed love and commitment to each other by sharing their possessions, eating together, and reminding themselves of Jesus' death and resurrection. It was so wonderful, so liberating! Nothing would ever be the same! Would it?

....

Thank you, Lord, for the family of God. Teach me to love the church, to pray for it and have faith for it to be hugely influential in my nation.

Read Joel 2:28–32: the promise of Pentecost.

WV

God's family

You are a chosen people, a royal priesthood, a holy nation, a people belonging to God, that you may declare the praise of him who called you out of darkness into his wonderful light. Once you were not a people, but now you are the people of God.

When I was born again in 1953, becoming a Christian seemed a very individual affair. As I grew up happily in a Christian environment, I often heard references to 'my personal saviour', 'my conversion', 'my testimony', and was encouraged to seek God's will for my life, all of which are extremely important. But a crucial ingredient was missing: the context in which these things were to be worked out, the people of God, the church. Church was a place you went to, not a family you were part of. Sadly, a lot of Christians were lonely.

God has always wanted a people for himself who will live devoted to him and declare his glory by their lives. He chose Israel initially for this, and, as their history unfolded, he brought prophets on to the scene to remind them that he intended to widen the scope of his blessings to those outside Israel; his light was coming to the nations! From all around the world people would be called out of darkness into light, into the *ekklesia*, the church. God is relational: he loves community.

God chooses individuals like stones, and loves to build them together into a 'spiritual house'. To him, each is 'chosen and precious'. Together, we are transformed into a 'holy nation'. A fundamental change has taken place; we have a new identity, 'the people of God'! Together we find new purpose, which is 'to declare the praise of him who called us', no longer living merely for ourselves.

Now the work begins: learning to relate as citizens of heaven! We need one another, just as a body needs arms and legs and head and heart. We need one another's differing gifts. There is a lot of 'one anothering' to do to know God and make a difference in this world.

....

Lord, teach me to love the body of Christ and play my part in it.

Read 1 Corinthians 12:12–31 to discover more about Christ's body, the church.

WV

Love one another

A new command I give you: Love one another. As I have loved you, so you must love one another. By this everyone will know that you are my disciples, if you love one another.

'What the world needs now is love, sweet love'; 'All you need is love'. Thousands of similar lyrics sound out every day from a million radios and CDs what we all believe and want to hear, that a little bit of love will change our lives. And of course they are right! Love is the most basic desire of the human heart, and without it, life is not worth living.

God knows that, and programmed us to be like that. God himself is in a love relationship. Jesus told his disciples, 'The Father loves the Son', and the Son and Holy Spirit love him and each other. From this community of love, Jesus came to show us what God is like. If there is one word that can explain the Father, it is 'love'. Only God's love can perfectly fill the empty space in our hearts.

But God's enemy, the devil, has perverted the true meaning of love. Instead of something essentially unselfish, and self-giving, he has managed to convince us that 'love' is all about self-gratification, self-fulfilment, 'me-centred'. A lot of what today is called 'love' is actually lust or greed.

Jesus modelled real love. It horrified the disciples when he took a towel and washed their feet: it was so demeaning! Yet he told them they must love each other in the same way! Love is not about preserving personal dignity. It's about putting other people first, honouring and valuing them, smoothing their path through life.

Self-fulfilment was not even a minor consideration to Jesus. He was consumed with obeying the Father by laying down his life. That is the essence of love. As we lay down our lives for one another, we will demonstrate the supernatural love of God.

....

Ask God to help you to love others, sacrificially, as he has loved you.

Read 1 John 3:16–18 for a definition of love.

WV

Forgive one another

Do not grieve the Holy Spirit… Get rid of bitterness, rage and anger… and… malice. Be kind and compassionate to one another, forgiving each another, just as in Christ God forgave you.

She screwed the tear-sodden handkerchief into a ball, and the tears continued to flow as she recounted the heartbreaking story of desertion by her husband, leaving her with two small children. Life was tough! Money was scarce. She was racked with the pain of rejection, eaten up with anger, and to top it all, where was God? She felt distant from him!

Together we read this scripture. Perhaps the root of her sense of distance from God had to do with 'grieving the Holy Spirit'. How? Harbouring anger, bitterness, malice can do that. How did she feel towards her husband? 'I want him to hurt the way he has hurt me.' Entirely understandable; but the Holy Spirit cannot live with malice.

'Get rid of it,' as it says here. How? 'Be kind, compassionate, forgiving one another…'

'*Forgiving*?!' she exploded. 'How unreasonable is that? I'm the injured party!'

'Do you recognize that you are harbouring anger and malice?'

'Yes.'

'And these grieve the Holy Spirit; they are sinful responses.'

'Yes.'

'Then you need to be forgiven too.'

She saw it: we can only forgive others as we see our own sin and need of forgiveness. She came to the cross and received forgiveness. Then she received healing, and the burden of grief began to lift.

Out of the deep clean well of forgiveness that now replaced the bitterness and malice, she drew out a bucketful of forgiveness for her husband. It was the beginning of a new attitude. Bitterness is destructive; forgiveness is Christ-like, and brings peace.

....

Ask God to show you if you are harbouring bitterness, rage, anger or malice towards others.

Read Matthew 18:21–35 to see how Jesus answered Peter's question about forgiveness.

WV

Bear one another's burdens

As we have opportunity, let us do good to all people, especially to those who belong to the family of believers.

My friend's husband died suddenly last winter at the age of 50. The shock was devastating; but perhaps even more devastating is learning to live without him indefinitely.

It is often the little things which highlight the deep sense of loss: like the day her ancient dishwasher broke yet again. Later the same day my friend returned home to find the kitchen awash because the washing machine had developed a hole in the drum, and the tumble drier had also ceased functioning! After a good cry, my friend went to a shop and ordered three new appliances, wondering how she was going to pay for them. The next day a letter came from a friend explaining that a large amount of money had been deposited in her bank account: enough to pay for all three new appliances!

God cares so tenderly for us, right down to specific details, but he does it through human beings who are sensitive to his whispers and who love each other. In Paul's day, the Pharisees loaded people down with guilt and law-keeping. Jesus came and lifted the burden of law off us by fulfilling the law himself. Then he gave a different law: 'Love your neighbour as yourself.'

'A trouble shared is a trouble halved' is an old cliché. It depends who you share your trouble with! But in the family of God there should be people with whom you can share your deepest needs and find support and encouragement. Small prayer groups are a good way of cultivating deep friendships and a context for loving care in practical ways. You might find that one needy person is overwhelming for an individual to care for, but a group can spread the load. Together we can carry burdens and show the love of Christ.

....

Thank you for your tender love for me, Lord. Please teach me to receive it from the family of God, and to give it.

To find practical advice on how to live with others, look up James 2:1–12.

WV

Serve one another

You... were called to be free. But do not use your freedom to indulge the sinful nature; rather, serve one another in love. The entire law is summed up in a single command: 'Love your neighbour as yourself.'

In this letter, Paul explains to the young Galatian church what it means to be free from the law. They had joyfully embraced the gospel, then along came some Jews who muddled them by insisting that it was necessary to continue to fulfil the law. These who so recently had been celebrating their freedom in Christ were now struggling under the law's onerous burdens.

Paul was furious. 'I am astonished', he wrote, 'that you are so quickly deserting the grace of Christ and turning to a different gospel!' He explained again the freedom of the gospel. But here he also spells out the pitfall of going to the other extreme—that freedom could become a licence to indulge in sin. 'Don't do that,' he urges, 'rather, serve one another in love.'

There are two other 'one anothers' that could happen if they continued to live by the law: destroying one another (v. 15) and provoking and envying one another (v. 26). Trying to live by the law fosters an atmosphere of accusation and competitiveness. It's better to look for ways to express love by serving one another. How? 'Live by the Spirit,' wrote Paul. It takes our focus off ourselves and motivates us to bless others.

A single mother, a new Christian who was hungry for Christian teaching, began attending church. Her unruly two-year-old would not stay in the crèche, but ran about distracting everyone. Earlier, an older woman had prayed at home about how she could serve the church. Perhaps prophesy? Share a reading? She saw her opportunity. Quietly she took the child out and cared for her all morning. The grateful mother was helped, and the rest of the church could listen in peace. Serving one another in love is a spiritual and practical occupation.

Help me, Lord, to be on the alert to see opportunities to serve my brothers and sisters in Christ.

Read Romans 12:6–13 and ask God to teach you how to exercise the gifts he gives you.

WV

Better than you?

Do nothing out of selfish ambition or vain deceit, but in humility consider others better than yourselves. Each of you should look not only to your own interests, but also to the interests of others. Your attitude should be the same as Christ Jesus.

The young pastor's wife knew she could not go on like this. Her attitude was so bad, it was poisonous! The trouble was, she was hostile to another woman in the fledgling church that she and her husband had started. The other woman seemed oblivious to the things that the pastor's wife found so irritating! She seemed loud and opinionated. Also her children were undisciplined and noisy, especially in meetings.

The pastor's wife tried to suppress her feelings of annoyance, but when she realized she was deliberately avoiding the other woman, she saw that her own ungodliness was becoming a problem. She knew she should value her, not judge her. One night, she decided to pray about it while her husband went to bed. She got on her knees and began a self-righteous prayer, listing all the understandable reasons for her frustrations. In fact she wrote out a list of things she felt were wrong with the other woman. As she read it she was startled to hear God say very clearly: 'You have just described yourself.'

She was overcome with conviction. It was clearly a case of seeing a 'speck' in the eye of another, but not being aware of the 'plank' in her own! (Matthew 7:3). She confessed her sin and repented. Then she began to ponder the command to 'Consider others better than yourself.' Before, it had been impossible. But now that she had a true perspective on herself, strangely it was not a problem any longer.

Later the two women met together and honestly faced their difficulties. Gradually they learned to give grace to each other and learned to love and value each other. True esteem can only come when we see ourselves, and each other, as God sees us.

....

Help me, Lord, not to have an inflated idea of my own importance. Help me to see other people the way you see them.

Read Matthew 7:1–5 and ask God to help you to see your own faults rather than the faults of others.

WV

Submit to one another

Submit to one another out of reverence for Christ.

Submission—the dreaded 'S' word! Churches have split over it, husbands and wives fall out over it, husbands have abused it, wives have rebelled against it—and we all think we know what it means!

Why is it so contentious? Because human nature is essentially not disposed to submit. Ever since Satan fell from his place in heaven where he became jealous of God and decided, 'I will make myself as the Most High' (Isaiah 14:14), he has fostered that same lust in the hearts of humankind. Consequently it is our proud boast, 'I will not submit to anyone!'

Then Jesus, the 'second Adam', came. He displayed a different spirit: 'By myself I do nothing; I seek not to please myself but him who sent me' (John 5:30). The devil did his utmost to deflect Jesus from this resolve. If he could get him to abandon his submission to the Father and act independently, the whole plan of salvation would be sabotaged, and the devil would triumph. But Jesus stayed humble and submissive to God all his life, and through the ordeal of the cross. 'Not my will, but yours be done.'

That's why the Enemy hates submission to God—it is powerful! So often we only view submission as a distasteful, archaic thing, to do with wives yielding to husbands. It is much wider than that! It is an ethos that should pervade the entire Church. God wants the whole church to be to him like a loving bride, displaying joyful obedience.

Submission to God is meaningless unless it is worked out in the area of human relationships. He does not want theoretical obedience. So we must learn to put aside our human arrogance and put on Christ-like humility. It is a learned attitude; every time a decision is made to submit to God and deny yourself, a victory is won.

....

Lord, I don't really want to submit to anyone; but I do want to submit to you as my King. Help me to work this out in the area of human relationships.

Read John 5:19–22 to discover Jesus' attitude.

WV

Spur one another on

Let us hold unswervingly to the hope we profess, for he who promised is faithful. And let us consider how we may spur one another on to love and good deeds.

Last Easter I ran a half marathon in Cape Town at the ripe old age of 58. I have always enjoyed running but had never run this distance (21km, or 13 miles) before. My friend Lindsey egged me on, 'Come on, let's do it together, it will be fun.' In a mad moment I signed up.

Of course, I intended to train; we both did. But complications set in. I injured my foot; then after six weeks of no running, I contracted a chest infection. Through all these obstacles, training was not just suspended, it was abandoned.

I had no intention of even trying. But the day before, Lindsey again urged me, 'Come on, at least make a start.' I did, and to my astonishment, I finished.

Several times during the race, I thought, 'If I were running on my own, there is no way I would have got this far!' I was running with several thousand others, all encouraging each other. The sense of camaraderie spurred us all on. Not only that, there were people lining the route handing out drinks and shouting encouragingly, 'Come on! You can do it! Keep going!'

We all need to be spurred on. We thrive on encouragement. It's often when you observe people taking initiatives to help others that you feel stirred to find ways to do the same. Maybe there are needy people in your church; or perhaps your church is setting up a programme to reach out to homeless people, or beginning a ministry in counselling, or starting an Alpha course. Let's consider how to support them: maybe we can join in the scheme, or give financially, or donate some equipment, or write a letter. What matters is that we do it together, rather than a few individuals battling on alone.

....

Encouragement is a gift of the Holy Spirit! How about asking God to make you an encourager?

Read Romans 12:3–8 to learn about the gifts God gives.

WV

Meeting together

Let us not give up meeting together as some are in the habit of doing, but let us encourage one another—and all the more as you see the Day approaching.

'You don't have to go to church to be a Christian'; 'I don't belong to any one church, I like to try different ones'; 'I listen to tapes'; 'I don't go to church, I watch the God Channel on TV'. People who make these sorts of comments have totally missed the point: church is not just a place you go to occasionally on a Sunday as an observer: the church is a community in which every person is an active participant. It is God's instrument for change in a sick society.

Meeting together is not only for your benefit. It is a place of power. When the saints are at prayer together, principalities and powers are watching, as God hears and answers. The presence of God is there, to save and to heal. It is a context in which we are changed and where we can grow; where we are stimulated to good works; where we find opportunities to express love to one another. It is a place where we can receive correction and instruction. Above all, it is a place of vibrant life!

You may say, 'My church isn't like that.' What should you be looking for in a church? If you read a letter like Titus, you will find that Paul expected certain things to be present. He addressed church leaders, instructing them to be faithful in marriage and keep their households orderly. He spoke to men and women, old and young, about their behaviour, that it should be pure and a good example. But the motivation came from their experience of the grace of God: they were saved by his great mercy! Church should be a context where the teaching leads us to appreciate our great salvation and, because of it, live in a way that honours God.

If you are reluctant to attend your church, ask yourself why. The time is short: be committed to a community of vibrant life!

....

Lord, I pray for the leadership and every member of my church, that we might be a holy, loving community, vibrant with the life of God.

Read Titus for a three-chapter snapshot of a New Testament church.

WV

Live at peace

Live in peace with each other... warn those who are idle, encourage the timid, help the weak.

Twenty years ago, a young Zulu was thrown into jail for being an ANC (African National Congress) activist. Recently married, lonely and afraid, he cried out to God for mercy. God met him powerfully and he is now a pastor of a church and at peace with Zulu, Africaans and white Christians.

Surely the ideal of every community is that the members can live amicably side by side, without tensions, fights and disagreements. But even in the most congenial places, with acres of space, peace can be lacking, because peace is not just to do with lack of noise or pleasant surroundings. In fact the peace that the apostle is talking about here is to do with attitudes to one another.

In Galatians Paul speaks of 'Jew and Gentile, male and female, bond and free'. The church was therefore inclusive of race, gender and status, a diverse community. In our day, some Christian leaders advocate deliberately targeting certain categories so as to build churches with the sort of people they are naturally comfortable with. But this is not true of the church portrayed in the New Testament. The church should be a rich mix of people from every walk of life, colour, social background, language group and economic status.

It was not easy in Paul's day. Social differences were very marked, and the Jews had centuries of exclusivity to deal with. James had to address some specific issues of rich people behaving in a thoughtless and superior way to poorer brothers and sisters. But it is possible when we remember that at the cross we are all equal, all sinners, all in need of grace. There is none righteous, no, not one, without the sacrifice of the lamb of God, who is sufficient and necessary for all.

....

Lord, I know I carry prejudices in my heart. Please give me a heart that reaches out regardless of money, class or accent.

Read Colossians 3:12–17 to discover more about how to find peace.

WV

Offer hospitality

Offer hospitality to one another without grumbling. Each of you should use whatever gift you have received to serve others, faithfully administering God's grace in its various forms.

What a rich passage this is! It offers a vivid snapshot of the early church. Peter reminds his readers that they no longer live for their own desires as they did in the past, but rather for the will of God. Time is running out—the best use they can make of it is to pray for, love and serve each other.

One of the most effective ways to love and serve each other is to offer hospitality. When we think of gifts in the body of Christ we may think of teaching, prophesying or musical gifts. But I heard one preacher declare that the gift he most valued, especially when beginning a new church, was hospitality.

We often underrate this gift, yet to welcome people into our home in the name of Jesus, is a powerful way of extending his love. In this passage Peter speaks of serving in the strength that God provides. The object is to bring praise to him. This means that hospitality is not primarily about flair for interior decorating or expensive food. It is not a vehicle for self-aggrandisement. Our homes, whether large or small, rich or poor, should be a place of shelter, contentment and growth.

In our first church there was a woman who lived in a very unpretentious home. Yet every Sunday she was on the look-out for newcomers. Somehow the food would always stretch and everyone had enough! Whoever went through her door felt loved and valued. Sitting at her table was an event! Consequently she had friends all over the world.

I know a single man given to hospitality, also a single woman, as well as many families. Hospitality enriches the life of the giver as well as the receiver and helps immeasurably to knit the body of Christ together.

....

Aquila and Priscilla invited Apollos to their home and explained the gospel to him. He went on to become a mighty preacher. You never know what might result from your kind invitation!

WV

Teach... as you sing psalms...

Let the word of God dwell in you richly as you teach and admonish one another with all wisdom, and as you sing psalms, hymns and spiritual songs with gratitude in your hearts to God.

Worship is primarily for God, but worship also builds us up. Singing has been an integral part of every revival. When God is near, people worship, and a major part of worship is in song. Charles Wesley wrote, 'Oh for a thousand tongues to sing my dear redeemer's praise!' His songs were full of doctrine expressed in a way that people could memorize. The task of the songwriter is a huge responsibility, because what people declare in song often stays in their hearts and minds and shapes their thinking.

It has rightly been said that we get a lot of doctrine from our hymns and songs. Therefore what we sing is very important! If we only sing very repetitive, superficial songs, our minds can be undernourished and our understanding shallow. But if we continually find ourselves singing declarations of glorious truth that stay with us through the day, our souls are edified as well as our minds informed concerning our faith.

In this passage in Colossians, Paul exhorts, 'Let the word of God dwell in you richly as you teach one another, admonish one another... and as you sing songs.' Our teaching, relating and worship must all be robustly based on the word of God.

Worshipping on your own must be a part of your individual devotion to God, but worshipping together as a church is hugely significant. We are expressing corporately our love, longing and loyalty to God. If we are led into God's presence, a spiritual dynamic takes place; we can come and receive from him, our hearts being soft and open. We are then in a place to receive fresh revelation, to be convicted of sin, to be healed or helped, affirmed and reassured. Do not come passively to worship: come expectantly.

....

Teach me, Lord, to worship you with all my heart, whether on my own or with the church.

Read Acts 4:23–31 to see Peter and John turning trouble into worship.

WV

Pray for one another

Confess your sins to each other and pray for each other so that you may be healed.

This passage is about people in a church being vulnerable with each other. Some are miserable, some are happy, some are sick, some are conscious of having sinned. All are admitting they can't make it on their own—they need each other.

Confessing our sins is not about beating ourselves up in public! It is more to do with being open and accountable to help us withstand temptation and keep clean. If you fall, ask God's forgiveness and ask someone you trust to hold you accountable.

Similarly, if you are depressed, don't keep it to yourself—ask for prayer. But if you are joyful, share the cause of your joy! Let others be encouraged!

In my church, people regularly ask the elders to anoint them with oil and pray for healing. There have been some remarkable instances of healing. Sometimes it has been rapid. In other cases, people have come week after week for prayer, and healing has taken place gradually.

I had coffee today with a woman who exercises a ministry of intercession. This is a hidden, sacrificial ministry. It is time-consuming, emotionally demanding and goes unrecognized and unacknowledged. But what a blessing to the church! I was humbled and encouraged as she falteringly told me how she had been praying for me. I had been totally unaware that this was the case, but I left blessed and built up.

Amazingly, we are told here that Elijah was a man 'just like us'. We don't tend to think of ourselves like him, able to call down fire, or pray for rain! But if we are in Christ, we are righteous, and 'the prayer of the righteous is powerful and effective'. So keep praying! It is more powerful than you think!

....

Use Paul's prayer in Ephesians 3:14–20 as a pattern to pray for others.

WV

God never planned for us to be isolated Christians. Although there are some believers forced into isolation by persecution, together with us, they are part of the glorious community described in the New Testament as the body and bride of Christ.

The body and bride image, which Paul uses to describe the church, challenges us to know Christ as intimately as a wife and husband know each other. Paul describes this knowing as 'a profound mystery' (Ephesians 5:32) in which Christ loves the church and gives himself up for her, making her holy, clean and radiant... without stain or wrinkle... but holy and blameless (Ephesians 5:25–27).

What part are you playing in this wrinkle-free bride? You are certainly a much-loved part, even if you are not always aware of how much God loves you. One of the wonderful things about a wedding is that the bride's main task is to delight her husband and respond to his love. She doesn't have an action plan or to-do list. All the hard work has gone on in the days and weeks before-hand. Now she is the focus of attention—radiant—the object of her new husband's adoration.

Play with this wedding imagery in your imagination; explore the 'profound mystery' that Paul writes about as you think about the love Christ has for you and for the church as a whole; let the words 'holy and blameless' transform your self-image and your attitude to the rest of your church... and the wider church, especially the parts of the wider church that you don't understand or with which you'd prefer not to be associated.

Over the next two weeks Jean Watson invites us to make a journey 'to live on the edge'. So often we stay in the centre of our comfort zone, surrounded by people and things we know and understand. But, as Jean suggests, when we live on the edge, we can see new horizons, new possibilities, fresh challenges.

Jesus lived on the edge—not in the comfortable company of the respectable majority, but with the marginalized. He invited unclean, stained and blame-ridden humanity to be his holy, radiant and blame-free bride. Invite Jesus to lead you out of your comfort zone to see new horizons over the next fortnight.

Living on the edge—securely

We do not lose heart. Though outwardly we are wasting away, yet inwardly we are being renewed day by day… we have a building from God, an eternal house in heaven… God… has given us the Spirit as a deposit, guaranteeing what is to come… we make it our goal to please him.

Have you ever noticed the borders or edges between one thing or place and another? You might like to look out of your window and notice the fences or hedges and what lies on either side of them; or the 'line' where land and sky, symbolic perhaps of earth and heaven, seem to meet.

Being on the edge, so to speak, of different vistas like those is probably a pleasant experience. But have you ever felt that you were living on the edge of a family or group—not completely 'in' for one reason or another? Or on the edge of your church because what is being taught doesn't seem to link with where you are on your spiritual journey? Or on the edge of the society around you because of what you believe and how you live? How does that kind of experience feel? Probably pretty uncomfortable. But can these uncomfortable situations prove to be good and worthwhile for us and others? That's what I hope we can explore in the coming two weeks.

For today, let's look at what this passage has to say about living on the edge and yet having a sense of security. There is implicit tension between 'wasting away' and, at the same time, 'being renewed', between what is happening to our bodies and what is going on in mind, heart and spirit. Can you identify with this tension? Are there any other uncomfortable feelings involved, for you, in living on this particular edge? What sources of security are mentioned or implied in the passage? Can you identify with these? Are there other reasons that make, or could make, this 'edge' a good place to be for you or others?

....

Turn your reflections and answers into praise and prayer.

Read Hebrews 13:5–6 and Philippians 4:13 for more possible sources of security in our 'edgy' situations.

JW

Walking with Jesus

As they talked and discussed these things with each other, Jesus himself came up and walked along with them... When he was at the table with them, he took bread, gave thanks, and broke it and began to give it to them. Then... they recognized him... They asked each other, 'Were not our hearts burning within us while he talked with us on the road and opened the Scriptures to us?'

Have you noticed the way courses have taken the place of big evangelistic meetings for introducing people to the Christian faith? The Emmaus course places the emphasis on walking with Jesus and learning from him in the context of ordinary daily life—travelling along, talking, arriving home, extending hospitality, having a meal—as the two disciples did in our passage. They were certainly living on the edge of hope and fear, understanding and bewilderment: 'they crucified him; but we had hoped'.

I find it very striking that, on joining the two walkers, Jesus did not draw attention to who he was and what had happened ('Hey guys, this is me—back from the dead!') Instead, he went with their agenda. He asked questions and listened as they retold what had happened—although he knew this perfectly well; and as they shared their feelings—disappointment, bewilderment, sadness.

Only then did he come in with the 'big picture' of these same events, saying, in effect, 'This isn't tragic or mysterious. It's what should have happened and is all for the best.' With scriptural back-up, he unfolded God's story as the ultimate context for theirs. Even when the disciples reached their destination, Jesus didn't take anything for granted; he waited for their invitation to go in and eat with them. At last, recognizing him by what he did with the bread at the table, they metaphorically kicked themselves: we should have realized sooner—when he said those things in that way—and our hearts were strangely touched!

....

Lead us on our journey to places of resurrection,
To dwellings of peace, to healings of wounds,
To joys of discovery.

RAY SIMPSON

JW

Living for Jesus

'The Spirit of the Lord is on me, because he has anointed me to preach good news to the poor. He has sent me to proclaim freedom for the prisoners and recovery of sight for the blind, to release the oppressed, to proclaim the year of the Lord's favour.'

How does anyone come to be living on the edge? Sometimes people are pushed into that situation by others or catapulted into a sense of being on the edge by severe trauma—bereavements, sudden losses and reversals of any kind, huge disappointment. How we see and respond to this will largely determine whether it proves ultimately beneficial or not in our lives and relationships.

Jesus, on the other hand, was called to live and work on the edge; he spent much of his time with all kinds of 'ordinary', marginalized, disadvantaged people. This made him very unpopular with the so-called respectable moral majority ('Why do you eat and drink with tax-collectors and "sinners"?' Luke 5:30). It can be the same today when Jesus' followers, are similarly called and make similar choices for his sake.

But despite the opposition and difficulties, there can be positive potential for us and for others coming out of that experience.

At the edge we see horizons denied to those who stay in the middle…
The edge is in fact always the centre of spiritual renewal.
RAY SIMPSON

Getting involved for Jesus' sake with people who are different from us and outside our normal comfort zone, can give rise to spiritual renewal—to growth, new insights and greater effectiveness. It was here at the edge with the poor and powerless that Jesus was welcomed and hence free to speak out, demonstrate and live out God's good news (Mark 12:37b).

....

Do I/does my church have any experience of living on the edge
with the poor, oppressed and marginalized? In terms of my town or
neighbourhood, who are they?

JW

Mundane and miracle

Now Moses was tending the flock of Jethro… and he led the flock to the far side of the desert and came to Horeb, the mountain of God. There the angel of the Lord appeared to him in flames of fire from within a bush.

In a sense, Moses' whole life was about living on the edge between mundane and miracle, beginning with his rescue as a baby and his life at Pharaoh's court as an adopted son. Today's passage is about one of the many 'between miracle and mundane' incidents in his life.

It happened on a day that must have begun much like any other for Moses at that time. As usual, he led the flock to a place where they could safely graze. Bushes—I imagine of the scrubby desert variety— must have been commonplace enough but suddenly there was one on fire but not burning up. So Moses is suddenly plunged from mundane into miracle. God's presence is evidenced first by fire symbolizing many things, including awesomeness, power and purity. Then God speaks.

When I was a small girl, I fully expected to see fairies at any moment and that my doll would turn into a real baby. Nowadays I understand why my expectations were never realized; and my 'miracles' are usually about the sudden transfigurations of the ordinary— those 'aha' moments of revelation, insight, delight.

'Ordinary' raindrops on an 'ordinary' window pane, when caught in bright sunlight, can suddenly look for all the world like diamonds. Artists have all their senses and imaginations open to such transformations and what they might mean or symbolize. Christians have every possible reason to be alert to wonder and meaning, but some of us fail to exercise our physical and spiritual imaginations.

Earth's crammed with heaven / And every common bush afire with God, / But only he who sees takes off his shoes, / The rest sit round and pluck blackberries (Elizabeth Barrett Browning)

....

Am I/is my church 'entirely open to God who works both through nature and through miracle' (John Stott, The Message of Acts)?

Try to find a Bible passage involving a 'mundane to miracle' transition that has some resonance in your experience.

JW

Between life and death

I have set before you life and death, blessings and curses. Now choose life, so that you and your children may live and that you may love the Lord your God, listen to his voice, and hold fast to him.

Romans 10:5–10 applies this passage to living under the leadership of Jesus. Choosing life means having a living, daily relationship with God, wanting to love him, listen to his voice and hold fast to him; and choosing death means the opposite. This choice confronts us the first time we make a decision to accept God's offer of forgiveness and new life. But it is also true that on a daily basis we can be heading for life (the way God wants us to live) or death—the many other ways we are free to go without God's presence or power or guidelines. Is my life evidencing which I have chosen and am constantly choosing?

We also live literally on the edge between life and death. Every day we are alive, we are dying physically; and, as we live in an uncertain world, we could face physical death at any moment. A poem I wrote 'To my doctor' if ever he has to tell me I'm terminally ill, ends like this:

> *Leave me, help me, to walk*
> *the tightrope of paradox*
> *living each day fully*
> *as if it were the last*
> *as if it were the first*
> *tying up loose ends*
> *weaving in fresh threads*
> *saying fond farewells*
> *hailing new beginnings.*

Our 'new beginnings' continue after death. So we can make the most of each moment of living on the edge between life and death now, with the prospect of life unshadowed by death or any sorrow still to come.

....

How does having a relationship with the Lord of life and death affect my willingness to live, or my way of living, on the edge between life and death?

JW

Who I am and who I am becoming

When I want to do good, evil is right there with me. For in my inner being I delight in God's law; but I see another law at work in the members of my body, waging war against the law of my mind.

Offer yourselves to God... and offer the parts of your body to him as instruments of righteousness.

These passages identify the fact that we, both as humans (flawed but made in God's image) and as Christians (flawed, made in God's image and under reconstruction) are living on the edge between the person we are and the person we have the potential to become.

As humans we have some intimations of God and of whom we could and should be—because of what theologians call common grace. The tension doesn't end when we become Christians. True, God is at work more directly in restoring his image in us, but many of us find that Paul's experiences of struggle between his 'old' and 'new' natures is reflected in our own. Are we, I wonder, as honest and open about it as he is?

A friend was at a Christian meeting where, after the talk, people were mingling and chatting. Someone came up and asked her how she was. Instead of giving a routine, 'Fine, thank you' or 'God is good' type of answer, she spoke very honestly, but without making a meal of it, of what was worrying and distressing her at the time. This drew a response of rapport and relief from her listener. It showed in her face and in her words, which went something like this: 'You're the first person here who doesn't seem to be absolutely fine—and that makes me feel that I am not the only person who's struggling.'

I believe my friend was honest with God and with herself about what it sometimes felt like to be living on the edge between heaven and earth and between who she was and who she was becoming. This gave her the freedom to be equally honest with others; fortunately she also had the discernment to use that freedom appropriately!

....

A day's retreat can be very useful in helping us to be more self-aware and honest about who we are and more hopeful about who we could become through all God's resources.

JW

Between joy and woe

Those who sow in tears will reap with songs of joy. Those who go out weeping, carrying seed to sow, will return with songs of joy, carrying sheaves with them.

The person writing Psalm 126 was in a very different place from the writer of Psalm 130. In the former, laughter is mentioned once and joy four times; in the latter there is crying out of the depths; there is sin, fear and—mentioned three times—waiting. Because the psalms reflect life in this world both for human beings and for God's people, they are often about living on the edge between joy and pain. As William Blake put it, 'Joy and Woe are woven fine, A clothing for the soul divine.'

Living on the edge between these two emotions and the experiences that give rise to them is obviously not easy. But can it prove also to be good and worthwhile in our lives and relationships? Joy can delight, release and expand us in all sorts of ways. But if we were to experience nothing else, might we not take things for granted and perhaps become superficial and selfish? What about woe? What's your experience of that and of living on the edge of both—as most of us do?

I and others have found that:

- woeful experiences can make us appreciate joyful ones—in the past, in the present or those to come—even more.
- in woeful experiences, we often find ourselves having to draw on all possible resources and hence becoming far more aware of all of these.
- through woeful experiences we can grow in qualities such as empathy, endurance, patience, gratitude and appreciation for small mercies and kindnesses, a sense of humour.
- experiencing joy and woe on earth can help us to make the most of earth while at the same time looking forward with greater eagerness to heaven.

Write your own psalm of joy or woe or both.

See 2 Corinthians 1:3–7; 4:16–18; and John 16:21–22 for more about the interface between joy and woe.

JW

Living between two kingdoms

'My kingdom is not of this world... My kingdom is from another place.'

'You have heard that it was said, "Eye for eye, and tooth for tooth". But I tell you... love your enemies and pray for those who persecute you, that you may be children of your Father in heaven.'

What catchphrases, slogans or words characterize the spirit of this age—life in the West lived without reference to God?

In what follows I am including what good humanists might have as their mottos as well as what materialists and self-absorbed people might convey: *Keep young and beautiful if you want to be loved. Realize your potential. Keep acquiring. Instant gratification. Look after yourself and your own. Act on the basis of mutual self-interest. Do just enough to stay within the law or at least to get away with your 'creative accounting'. Try not to do anyone any harm. Live life to the full. Always look on the bright side of life. Follow your heart. Be happy.*

Which of these or any others you can think of clash with biblical values and aims, and which echo them to a greater or lesser extent? Catchphrases, slogans or words that express biblical values might include: *Mercy and justice. Gentleness and meekness (not mildness!). Not being possessed by possessions. Extravagant generosity. Going the second mile. Purity of heart. Kindness. Love. Forgiveness. Active for the powerless and exploited. What would Jesus do? What does God expect? Where is God in this? How can I help to bring God's kingdom in—in this situation?*

How aware are you of your true kingdom—culture, values, behaviour, lifestyle—overarching and searchlighting the kingdom of this world? Jesus alone fully exemplified the culture, values, behaviour and lifestyle of God's kingdom while living on earth, but we follow in his footsteps, albeit with L-plates on.

....

Lord, help me to reflect the kind of heavenly mindedness that is of earthly use; and to be of earthly use in ways that will draw people into your kingdom on earth and in heaven.

JW

Between earth and heaven

[Jacob] had a dream in which he saw a stairway resting on the earth, with its top reaching to heaven, and the angels of God were ascending and descending on it... He... said, 'How awesome is this place! This is none other than the house of God; this is the gate of heaven.'

Our Bible passages describe two occasions when heaven broke through into earth in different ways. As you read them, did you notice the feelings and responses of those involved?

In the first, Jacob was awestruck, but not too awestruck to respond in a way that was typical of his nature: he made a bargain with God. He also set up a memorial, wanting to make this event a key moment, a turning point, in his life. In the second, the story of the transfiguration of Jesus, Peter and friends felt frightened, but in Peter's case not too frightened to respond in a way that was typical of him: he made a spontaneous and ill-thought-out but generous, warm-hearted suggestion about building tents for the celebrities and staying there—holding on to the experience, perhaps.

We sometimes use the phrase, 'it was a little taste of heaven', but only when something is so fabulous, right and special that we instinctively feel it prefigures heaven. How have you felt and responded to little touches of heaven on earth? What about a newborn child, an absolutely perfect flower, or a dream, moment of insight or wonderful experience of God's presence...?

In John Bunyan's *The Pilgrim's Progress*, when Christian and Hopeful get into Beulah, they catch a glimpse of heaven's golden streets and buildings of pearls and precious stones, and 'feel sick', smitten by the sudden splendour of it all and their longing to be there. This is a picture, I think, of how it feels for us to be living on the edge of earth and heaven—feeling both the pain of the former and the joy of the latter. What is your experience in this area?

....

Lord, help me not to miss glimpses of heaven and your glory here and now on earth.

JW

Where I've been and where I'm going

Christ Jesus: Who, being in very nature God... made himself nothing, taking the very nature of a servant, being made in human likeness. And being found in appearance as a man, he humbled himself and became obedient to death... Therefore God exalted him to the highest place... that at the name of Jesus every knee should bow.

Jesus' life perfectly illustrates living on the edge between the past and the present. Our passage summarizes this but if you want to read of Jesus' actual words and deeds in this connection, look at Matthew 16:21–28; 26:52–53; John 13:1, 31—14:9; Mark 14:61–62.

The creed, based on Bible passages, summarizes Jesus' past and future in its distinctive way, but it can be challenging to try and rewrite Bible verses and credal statements in our own words. With this past and future focus particularly in mind, we might write something like this: *Jesus came from heaven, from a place of highest privilege and responsibility in his Father's house. He laid aside his status, lived as a human being, showing and teaching us how to live under God's rule. He experienced pain, abuse, injustice and was put to death. He rose again to take up the reins of the kingdom he had established on earth, until the time should come for the final outworking of justice and love in the new eternal heaven and earth.*

Although Jesus was fully aware of his past and his future, he was able to be fully present at every moment of his life, savouring it for all it was worth, and following his calling faithfully. He was fully receptive to people, contributing generously by being, telling and living out God's good news, which applied to his and their past, present and future.

Are you overfocused on the past or the future, or both? Is this an area where reflection, talking to someone else, action—or all three—might be healing or releasing in your daily life and relationships?

....

Lord of my past, present and future, help me, starting today, to live on the edge between where I've been and where I'm going—while learning to be fully present for and to each person and situation.

JW

Between grief and hope

Mary stood outside the tomb crying. As she wept, she bent over to look into the tomb and saw two angels in white, seated where Jesus' body had been.

She came to find him where
she knew he would be.
'He is not here!'
Cheated even of these
last rites, in tears
she stumbled off
into the barren plain.
There she heard
him speak her name...
I weep at my empty
tombs of loss, disillusion:
but who is that calling
to me from the garden?

All kinds of things affect the way we grieve—our temperament; the relationship we had with the deceased; the way that person died; our overall framework in terms of family, friends, work, means of support.

Temperamentally, Mary seems to have been an emotional and responsive person, not afraid to express her love publicly and risk censure. The way Jesus died must have distressed her hugely. She owed her healing and new life to him. In her society at that time, she would not have had much in terms of status and protection and her overall framework was limited. In her loss, she sought the grave of the person who meant so much to her. But when she heard her name and looked round, she got far more than she could ever ask or think—not the grave but the garden; not death but life. No longer was she weighed down by loss and helplessness, but buoyed up by hope, meaning, purpose. Can you draw parallels with your own experiences of grief and hope?

....

Lord of hope, thank you for all the people, places and ways through whom and through which you have brought me past hope and I ask now for present hope in this situation...

JW

Between faith and doubt

'Unless I see the nail marks in his hands and put my fingers where the nails were, and put my hand in his side, I will not believe it… My Lord and my God!'

Can you think of people in the Bible who were torn between faith and doubt at some time in their lives? Some that spring to my mind are, in the Old Testament: Abraham, Moses, David, many of the prophets; and in the New: Peter, John the Baptist, as well as the apostle in our passage today—Thomas. Since New Testament times, many Christians—including some very well-known ones—have had similar experiences.

Doubt can result from our temperament, from our experiences and our responses to them. And there's a big difference between honest doubt and chronic—habitual, determinedly chosen—pessimism. Thomas was an honest doubter. Jesus did not condemn him; and what a lot we learn from his struggles with faith and doubt! He was honest about his feelings. He wanted evidence, but he was willing to be convinced by it, and when convinced, he admitted it wholeheartedly—uttering one of the most succinct and complete declarations of faith in the New Testament—one that has been echoed by millions ever since.

For Thomas faith came through his physical senses—he saw, heard, spoke to, touched Jesus. For us faith can dispel doubt through our spiritual senses. How do we exercise and experience these? Through relating to God in prayer and worship; reading and meditating on the Bible, 'reading' the 'book' of nature—God's creation; reflecting on God's presence and prompting in the past; talking and listening to other Christians…

Bask in being among the 'blessed' who have not had the evidence that Thomas had, and yet, following his example—believe, cry out, 'My Lord and my God', and act in faith on that creed.

....

Lord, wherever I am on the spectrum between faith and doubt, I do believe; help my unbelief. Help me to maintain an honest, receptive dialogue with you and a humble, teachable attitude—and so to keep learning and growing in the school of faith.

JW

Between strength and weakness

Though outwardly we are wasting away, yet inwardly we are being renewed day by day… we fix our eyes not on what is seen, but on what is unseen.

These passages identify various strengths and weaknesses and our experiences of living with both. In 2 Corinthians 4, Paul refers to feet of clay; being hard pressed but not crushed; carrying around Jesus' death and life; wasting away yet being renewed. In 2 Corinthians 11 and 12, he speaks of being well-born, well-educated and privileged but also of having a thorn in the flesh. Can you identify with any of that?

We all live between strength and weakness. Are we honest and humble before God about our strengths and weaknesses—willing to see them as he does and to let him transform and use them as he wants to?

Let's think about weaknesses first of all. Are you aware of yours? As well as qualities of character, there is the fact that we are growing older each day and, also, we can never be sure of what is round the corner in terms of health or illness, happy events or traumas. Whichever of these you might classify as weaknesses, they can all become ways of growing and learning. Can you illustrate this from your own life?

What do you see as your strengths? I have listened to sermons in which the preacher has held up cards with words on them such as: *going to church*; *being a good person*; *education*; *status*; *money*… These cards are then dramatically torn up to make the point that none of those things gain us forgiveness and a relationship with God. Quite right too. But all these, though useless in terms of winning us favour with God, can become useful strengths when we accept God's gift of forgiveness and new life and put all our resources under his leadership.

This is what happened with Paul. As a follower of Jesus, his scholarship, communication and reasoning skills, wholeheartedness and the rest, were able to be used in the work to which he was called.

....

Lord, these are my strengths and weaknesses, as I see them… How do you see them? Is there anything I am unaware of? Anything that hasn't been given to you for changing and using?

JW

Confidence and humility

When I consider your heavens, the work of your fingers, the moon and the stars, which you have set in place, what are mere mortals that you are mindful of them, human beings that you care for them?

'You come of the Lord Adam and Lady Eve,' said Aslan. 'And that is both honour enough to erect the head of the poorest beggar, and shame enough to bow the shoulders of the greatest emperor on earth' (C.S. Lewis, *Prince Caspian*, Collins).

In the book circle I belong to, we have been reading *A Brief History of Nearly Everything*, by Bill Bryson. We all thought it remarkable, but some also used words such as 'scary' and 'frightening'. I found myself feeling insignificant when I put my tiny little self within all the antiquity, vastness and complexity of the cosmos; and significant when I reminded myself of the biblical truth that the God who designed and is involved and active in all of that, knows, loves and has plans for his creation and everyone and everything in it, including me.

Bill Bryson's book doesn't make God redundant. Only if we believe in a God of the gaps—the gaps in our understanding of the world and life—is there a danger of 'losing' God as he is increasingly squeezed out as our knowledge increases. But if God made, maintains and is active in every part of the universe, then becoming more aware of how things work and interconnect just serves to increase our understanding of him. To be able to talk and listen to this God as our father, ruler and friend is both humbling and affirming.

1 Peter 3:15 says, 'Always be prepared to give an answer to everyone who asks you to give the reason for the hope that you have.' Does anyone ever ask the reason for the hope that we have? If not, are we living in a way that would raise such questions? If anyone *is* asking these questions, does the tone of our answer reflect what Peter goes on to say: 'Do this with gentleness and respect, keeping a clear conscience'?

....

Lord, I pray for a right balance between confidence and humility, and for genuine confidence and humility—not cockiness and brashness on the one hand or passivity and inferiority on the other.

JW

David, the Shepherd King, is the focus of the next two weeks' Bible readings. He is also an example of someone who 'lived on the edge'. As the youngest, he was on the outer edge of his family—marginalized and almost forgotten when Samuel comes to appoint the next king from among Jesse's sons.

He waits in the desert for God to call him into active service—again on the edge, before moving to court to play his harp to soothe a troubled king. Even at court, he is on the edge, watching and responding to the king's mood changes. He is catapulted from the edge to centre stage when confronted with Goliath, demonstrating God's preference for the youngest, smallest and most insignificant when he chooses to bestow greatness.

Jesus showed the same preference when he said, 'Whoever welcomes this little child in my name welcomes me; and whoever welcomes me welcomes the one who sent me. For he who is least among you all—he is the greatest' (Luke 9:48).

Paul understood this basic principle when he explained: 'God chose the foolish things of the world to shame the wise; God chose the weak things of the world to shame the strong' (1 Corinthians 1:27).

Have you grasped this way of looking at the world? We are surrounded by pressures to think in the opposite way to God: we are surrounded by a culture that aspires to wealth, strength, beauty, intelligence, speed... We look for the spectacular, but often God is at work in small and secret ways, with poor, marginalized, weak people. And when he does reveal his spectacular power through miracles, it is rarely among the wealthy, strong, 'beautiful' people in the West, but with the hungry and disadvantaged who have to put their hope in God, rather than in an NHS, and whose hope is not squashed by cynicism.

Over the next two weeks, as you study David's life with all its inadequacies and failings as well as strengths, remember that David was described as 'a man after God's heart' (1 Samuel 13:14; Acts 13:22). Ask God to help you get to know his heart as you consider the life of this man whom God chose.

Knowing God by his Spirit

'People judge others by what they look like, but I judge people by what is in their hearts.'... As soon as David came, the Lord told Samuel, 'He's the one!'... the Spirit of the Lord took control of David and stayed with him from then on.

'I don't have a job. I'm just a housewife.' How many times have you heard that, or even said something like it yourself? 'I'm just a pensioner' or 'I am just a secretary' or 'I just do this and that, nothing special.' In an age of impressive job titles and assertiveness training, of authorities and experts, we often compare ourselves unfavourably with others. Many of us feel very ordinary. Insignificant.

That is certainly what Jesse and the family thought of the youngest son. Born of older, weary parents, he was an extra, an afterthought. Babysitting the sheep in the countryside is the task where he would be least nuisance. So dispensable is that he, when the great prophet Samuel arrives in Bethlehem on a tricky mission from God to appoint a successor to the ill-fated King Saul, no one thinks to call the boy to the family gathering. He is quite forgotten until Samuel, coming unsuccessfully to the last of the impressive line of seven candidates asks, 'Are these all the sons you have?'

It is only then that this still unnamed son makes an appearance in the biblical story. There, in front of his puzzled father, his humiliated brothers, and the relieved prophet, the Spirit of the Lord comes upon David. He experiences God as never before. God's hand is on him. God is the one who knows him intimately, who sees past politics and prejudice. He knows God as the one who has chosen him to be king, not because of what he can do, but for who he is. God sees his heart. He is not insignificant. His first difficult task is to await God's timing, but as he returns to his mundane, obscure activities, he knows he has a God-given destiny to fulfil.

···

I am not 'just' anything: I am chosen. If I am God's child, his Spirit is in me. I know him better as I respond in obedience.

Read John 14:15–17 to remind yourself of the Spirit's presence and help and guidance.

FB

Knowing God in the waiting

'A man named Jesse… has a son who can play the harp,' one official said. 'He's a brave warrior, he's good-looking, he can speak well, and the Lord is with him.'… David went to Saul… Saul liked him so much that he put David in charge of carrying his weapons.

'I am chosen. I am special. I have a divine destiny to fulfil.' Great words. True words. Only it doesn't always feel like that when your child has just been sick for the fourth time, or your boss is being particularly unreasonable, or your illness drags on interminably. 'It's not meant to be like this,' you say to yourself. 'All this stuff—work, routine, responsibilities, disabilities, people—it all gets in the way of me being what God has called me to be. If only I could get rid of it I would serve God better.'

As the newly anointed David returns to his sheep, everything has changed and nothing has changed. He can only wait until God's plan unfolds further. And it happens quite unexpectedly. No one could have imagined that David's hobby would be the means by which he would be thrust from obscurity into court life. He exchanges a shepherd's crook for a musician's harp. His playing brings calm to the tormented king. When his fingers move over the strings, Saul's spirit is massaged from madness to solace.

We can only guess at David's feelings as he spends his days bringing healing to the rejected king. Where is the Lord in it all? If David is to replace Saul, wouldn't it be better if God left him to descend into insanity unchecked? Has he been taken there to be tantalized by all he might have, but not yet?

But this is not just an interlude before David will 'come into his own'. God is using him there even as he is preparing him. The harp playing, like the shepherding, are opportunities for David to grow in his understanding and to demonstrate his faithfulness to God. These are not obstacles; they are stepping stones in his path of obedience.

....

Waiting is hard, and we can forget that, in the meantime, there is work to be done! How can I live out God's calling to me today?

FB

Knowing God in the battles

'I've come out to fight you in the name of the Lord All-Powerful. He is the God of Israel's army and you have insulted him too!… the Lord doesn't need swords and spears to save his people. The Lord always wins his battles and he will help us defeat you.'

'What has happened to you? You used to be normal before you became a Christian,' my friend's mother once told him. Being a Christian can be a lonely experience when we are the only ones in our families or social circles. Or it may be that our work pressurizes us to compromise our Christian values of honesty and integrity: 'Yes, but it is only a white lie…'

As we face a range of challenges to our Christian faith, from gentle teasing to aggressive hostility, we may draw encouragement from this encounter between David and Goliath. David, 'only a boy' takes his stand before a terrified, demoralized nation and against an arrogant brutish one. Unable and unwilling to don conventional soldier's dress or to pretend to be anyone other than he is, he faces the enemy with nothing other than conviction and belief in the living God, a stone and a sling. This simple calm faith amid the daily bullying and panic catches everyone unawares. In no time, the one who threatens the future of the people of Israel is dead.

In making the story our own, it is important to remember that Goliath does not represent any old big thing that intimidates us. He stands for everything and everyone that mocks and dishonours the living God. That is what gives David his holy fury and confidence: Goliath has defied the Lord by imagining that might is right and that God is incapable or unwilling to save his people. Sadly even they believe the lies—and it takes a 'non-professional' devoted worshipper whose vision is full of the invisible God, rather than the grisly enemy before him, to demonstrate the reality of the sovereign rule of Almighty God.

....

Pray that, in the battles you face today, God's honour may be uppermost in your mind.

Read Ephesians 6:10–18 and put on God's armour.

FB

Knowing God in friendship

Jonathan said, 'Go in peace! The two of us have vowed friendship in God's name, saying, "God will be the bond between me and you, and between my children and your children forever!"'

Is friendship a luxury or a necessity? Many things militate against friendship. We are busy and fatigued. We are frightened to be open and vulnerable. We often see intimacy in sexual terms and so pursue it principally in marriage and family life with variable success. We can pay counsellors to listen to us.

The friendship between David and King Saul's son Jonathan is strange and unexpected. Jonathan is a prince, the oldest son and close to his father. David is a shepherd, the youngest of eight and often forgotten. Jonathan's home is a palace with servants, while David the country boy is himself a servant at court. Jonathan is the natural heir to his father's throne, but David is God's anointed heir. One of the joys of friendship is when affection is stronger than so-called incompatibilities.

This friendship is strong. It flourishes not in carefree leisurely pursuits, but in dark places where everything seems to militate against it. 'Jonathan made a covenant with David because he loved him as himself.' This loyalty is enormously costly for Jonathan, pulled as he is between a commitment of emotional intimacy to David and filial duty to his father who makes numerous attempts to kill David.

This friendship is strategic. It is God's way of ensuring that David fulfils his call. With so much persecution, David could give up and return to his sheep, but God uses Jonathan, the one who stands to lose the most, to confirm to him that he is God's choice as king. Eugene Peterson, in his brilliant book on David writes, 'bound in the covenant of Jonathan's friendship, David is protected, none of Saul's evil gets inside him.' Not only David's future, but that of God's people depends on this gracious, life-giving friendship.

....

'Friendship is a much underestimated aspect of spirituality… Like the sacramental use of water and bread and wine, friendship takes what's common in human experience and turns it into something holy.' (Eugene Peterson)

FB

Knowing God in persecution

'I'll let the Lord decide which one of us has done right. I pray that the Lord will punish you for what you're doing to me, but I won't do anything to you.'

Remember the story in the news of the betrayed wife who cut one sleeve off each of her husband's many suits and dispersed his precious wine collection to everyone in the village with their milk delivery? I find myself smiling as I visualize her outrage and his reaction, because somehow I feel he deserves it. There is a sense of justice about his humiliation and it serves as a rallying cry for other victims of selfishness. 'Revenge is sweet' is the popular saying, but is it true?

David is being hounded and persecuted by King Saul. Hiding in the harsh, inhospitable desert, survival is his daily battle, his weekly chore. Then one day, he is given the opportunity to end the torture, to act in self-defence, to facilitate God's plans to make him king. Saul uses the cave where David and his men were hiding to withdraw from his army of 3,000 for a private toilet stop. Yet to everyone's amazement, David does no more than cut a piece of his robe, and even then is overcome with guilt. Once Saul has left the cave, David calls to him, expressing his anguished 'Why?' at the way he is being vilified, and casting their relationship before the Lord for judgment. In the poignant exchange that follows he demonstrates his maturing spirituality and trust in God's ways.

David understands that revenge may feel instinctive, and yet it is illegitimate and ineffective. He refuses to allow Saul's evil to so burrow into his own soul that he can only retaliate with bitterness and violence. In all his heartache and fear, he chooses to trust God as judge and the only one with the right to punish. The effect is complete disarmament of the paranoid terrifying aggressor into a penitent, weeping man (albeit temporarily).

....

David does not let evil get the better of him, but gets the best of evil by doing good. How can I apply this to the situations that challenge me today?

Read 1 Peter 2:19–25. What did Jesus' unjust suffering achieve for us?

FB

Knowing God when sense is lacking

[David told Abigail,] 'I praise the Lord God of Israel! He must have sent me to meet you today. And you should also be praised. Your good sense kept me from taking revenge and killing innocent people.'

'I thought God had helped me deal with that sin. Why am I doing it again? It's so silly. I am back to square one.' Do you, like me, get frustrated with yourself?

Only yesterday we were admiring David's stand against revenge. One chapter later, we are confronted by an avenging David. He takes offence at the 'fool' Nabal, who won't acknowledge the protection he and his men have given Nabal's shepherds in the brigand-infested desert. All it needs is an invitation to the workers' party. Compared to the trauma inflicted on him by Saul this is nothing, but something snaps and David forgets about trusting God as judge. He plans a bloodbath for every man associated with Nabal.

But it doesn't happen. Is it because David remembers the lesson about spiralling violence? Is it that through prayer he understands this is not God's will? Does he gain a sense of perspective when he thinks of Saul's cruelty? No. He is stopped in his tracks by the beautiful, intelligent Abigail, wife of Nabal. Abigail brings the mouth-watering banquet and the recognition he craves. More importantly, she heals his wounds by embodying a gentle reminder from God. She assures him that his life 'will be bound securely in the bundle of the living by the Lord' (NIV) because of his calling to be king and his work in 'the Lord's battles'. The sword falls from his hand as she commends him for not taking revenge that has not been divinely commissioned. He is enabled to see things from God's long-term perspective once again.

I am sometimes taken aback when minor incidents rather than major challenges cause me to stumble. I desperately need 'Abigails' to whisper God's encouragement and grace lest I fall further.

....

Don't think that you go round in repetitive circles with regard to sin. Imagine instead a corkscrew, as the Spirit moves deeper into your life tackling sin and making you holy.

FB

Knowing God in new challenges

All the tribes of Israel approached David... and said, 'Look at us—your own flesh and blood! In time past when Saul was our king, you were the one who really ran the country. Even then God said to you, "You will shepherd my people Israel, and you'll be the prince."'

How do you respond to new challenges? Do they excite or terrify you? Do you bound up to new responsibilities with relish and confidence, or do you lie awake at night wishing that your stomach would stop churning and you could go back to the way things used to be? Do you shout 'Yes, this is what I was made for!' or do you whimper 'I can't do this; it's just not me'?

With Saul's death in battle, David faces a profound change of role and lifestyle. For ten years he's been a frustrated, terrified fugitive on the edge of society, waiting for God's promise that he would be king.

Yet David's long apprenticeship in the wilderness has deepened his understanding that God's work has to be done in God's way. After a time of genuine and open grief for Saul and his friend Jonathan, he enquires of the Lord about his next step. It results in the people of Judah anointing him king. It is only seven years later, that the northern tribes of Israel ask him to rule over them too, recalling the Lord's promise that he would 'shepherd' his people.

That word 'shepherd' is significant. His long-awaited vocation as ruler is not a break from the past. It will require all the caring, nurturing and leadership skills he has developed from his youth. Nothing from the previous troublesome years is wasted or disregarded. David's rule will reflect what he has learned over time from having the Lord as his shepherd.

David has understood that his power is not for his own amusement. It is God-given. As shepherd and musician, fugitive and now king he is in, and under, God's sovereign will and purpose.

We need the Spirit's steady ongoing work of making us like King Jesus. It takes time, but no experience is ever wasted.

Think of the Christian life as a marathon and not a sprint; then read Hebrews 12:1–3.

FB

Knowing God in anger

**David got angry because of God's deadly outburst against Uzzah…
David became fearful of God that day and said, 'This Chest is too hot
to handle. How can I ever get it back to the City of David?'**

'I was only trying to help!' There is something infuriating when our
best efforts to do the right thing land us in trouble. We try to bring reconciliation between warring parties and find ourselves attacked. We
suggest a new way of doing things at church only to be misunderstood.
We enthuse about our faith at work and meet with ridicule and
ostracism. 'Lord,' we say in frustration, 'I am doing this for you: why
don't you make it work out?'

David prays like this, only he is furious. He arranges for the ark of the
covenant to be brought from decades of obscurity to the very centre of
national life. In bringing this physical symbol of God's presence to the
new capital Jerusalem, King David wants everyone to recognize and
celebrate God's supreme rule. Then suddenly, the joyous procession is
interrupted when the oxen pulling the cart bearing the chest stumbles
and Uzzah tries to stop it from falling to the ground. This simple move
is the death of him; he dies because of 'his irreverent act' (NIV).

If we find this hard to understand, how much more excruciating it
is for David, whose well-meaning project ends in incomprehensible
tragedy! His anger turns to fear: this God is dangerous! Yet David is suf-
ficiently honest and alive to God to know that he can express his anger
openly.

His fear does not lead to timidity but to a new reverent obedience.
Three months later, when David returns to collect the ark, it is carried
on poles by consecrated Levites, rather than an impersonal cart, as the
Lord had instructed Moses years before. These are indeed different
times, and yet the awe and respect in dealing with the holy things of
God is an unchanging obligation.

....

*Teach me to be honest before you, Lord, when I don't understand
what you are doing. Yet in my candour, let me not become familiar
or manipulative.*

FB

Knowing God in worship

[David] was dancing for the Lord with all his might... when [Michal] saw David jumping and dancing for the Lord, she was disgusted... David told her... 'The Lord chose me, and I was celebrating in honour of him.'

When you are in love, you forget everyone and everything around you. When you are cynical, lovers are infuriating and pathetic.

David's timely reminder of the dangerous aspect of God's holiness following Uzzah's death did not dampen his enthusiastic worship when the ark of the Lord was finally brought to Jerusalem. Rather it sharpened his wonder. David could not contain himself. He was so 'in love' with the almighty God who had selected him as ruler and was actually willing to live among his sinful people that his delight became a dance.

Flinging aside his kingly robes and the pompous dignity that would remind all his subjects who was boss, David 'danced before the Lord'. Here was total self-forgetfulness, a joyful self-abandonment. He didn't need external props to reassure him. His focus was on God.

Michal, David's wife, observed from a window and despised him. She had once been very much in love with him, but years of suffering as a pawn between him and her father King Saul had left her bitter. Perhaps because of her scars, she clung to the only thing she had left— her royal position. She could not understand how David would not use this magnificent occasion to underline his own kingly dignity, to make his god serve him. His exuberance seemed excessive and unnecessary.

Watching other people in adoration is disconcerting and probably unhelpful. If worship is giving all that we are to him, outwardly it will look very different, because we are distinct characters. But worship is looking at God. Discussion and debate, bitterness and cynicism may stop us throwing ourselves in wonder and thanksgiving and praise before the Holy One who loves us and has chosen us and is with us.

....

'It's all about you, Jesus.'
Remind yourself of the special
love God has poured out on
you, and thank him for it.

Use Ephesians 1:3–14 as a
springboard for praise.

FB

Knowing God in prayer

David went into the tent he had set up for the sacred chest. Then he sat there and prayed: 'Lord All-Powerful, my family and I don't deserve what you have already done for us, and yet you have promised to do even more.'

Sometimes in my enthusiasm to do 'something beautiful for God', I can end up treating him like a respected but incapable elderly relative. I get so carried away with what I am doing for him that all the responsibility seems to rest on my shoulders and I forget who is in control.

Having established himself as king, David decides that God's ark needs a home at least as majestic as his. He confides in Nathan the prophet, who has no doubt of his sincerity, and encourages him in his idea of building a temple. However, that night God speaks to Nathan of a much greater plan, which blows David's mind when Nathan tells him.

'David,' he says, 'what is most important is not what you can do for me; I don't need anything. Let me remind you what I have done for you, bringing you from tending sheep to being ruler of Israel. Look at what I am doing for you now—and listen to what I am going to do for you: I will make your name great and build you an everlasting dynasty.'

Overwhelmed by the lavish generosity of God, David goes and just sits before the Lord. His understanding of God and his ways have expanded and he expresses his devotion and desires in prayer. No longer 'doing' or 'planning', he simply pours out the wonder and worship of his heart.

David's lesson is not only pertinent to those who busy themselves 'pleasing God', but also to those who feel useless because of circumstance or disability. God's gracious ways are more marvellous than our plans. This is not a call to passive inactivity, but a reminder that what he does for us is more important and awesome than anything we do for him. Attentiveness to his will is key.

···

Are you aware of changes to your life since you first came to know Jesus? Praise God for who he is and what he has done.

Read Philippians 2:12b–13 to see a balance between God's activity and ours.

FB

Knowing God in promises

**David thought, 'I wonder if any of Saul's family are still alive. If they are, I will be kind to them, because I made a promise to Jonathan.'...
David said [to Mephibosheth], 'Don't be afraid... I'm going to give back the land that belonged to your grandfather Saul... you will always eat with me at my table.'**

Last weekend, my father gave me a 'promise ring', which had been a gift from his grandfather to his future wife before they were even engaged. 'It's around 115 years old,' he said. I wish it could tell me the family and social history it has witnessed from the days before Freud, Marie Curie, and Peter Rabbit. What I find especially poignant is the dignity and patience of their courtship in days when a man would have to be able to provide for his sweetheart before he could marry her. As I touch it now on my middle finger, I feel kinship with strangers. It is because they kept their promise that I have been given life.

Promises are in the air David breathes. God's covenant love has kept him alive. God's promise that he would be king maintained his openness to the Lord's purposes through the wilderness years. The God-given friendship with Jonathan, which sustained him through Saul's opposition, was crowned with a declaration of loyalty and care not only to each other but also to their families, whatever happened.

So David's search for Mephibosheth, Saul's natural living heir, is a beautiful story of a promise remembered, of the king reaching out to a man who calls himself a dog because of his disabilities and his precarious political position. It is a tale of unpretentious extravagance as David brings his friend's forgotten son to his own dinner table. The situation has changed since David first made that commitment. Others might have seen Mephibosheth as a threat and considered it sensible to be kind at a distance. Yet David, who basks in the Lord's unfailing covenant to him, extends grace with vulnerability, but without reserve.

....

'Love one another as I have loved you.' Are there promises that I have made that I need to remember to keep?

Read 1 Corinthians 13 as a template for love.

FB

Knowing God in sinfulness

David said, 'I have disobeyed the Lord.' 'Yes, you have!' Nathan answered. 'You showed you didn't care what the Lord wanted. He has forgiven you, and you won't die. But your newborn son will.'

'I really can't stand her: she is so opinionated, so judgemental. She always talks as though she knows best.' I was trying to put into words all the reasons why the relationship with my boss wasn't working. My friend listened quietly through the tirade and then smiled: 'She sounds a whole lot like you, then.'

It is strange, isn't it, how I make allowances for my own faults, and call my own failings by other names! I have very good reasons why I speak and act in certain ways, but when I see that same behaviour reflected in others, I am merciless. Painful though it may be, I need others to confront me with myself.

That's what Nathan does for David, in God's name. He tells the story of a wealthy man, who had everything, stealing a pet lamb from the poor man, who had nothing. Any sheepy tale would be bound to touch an ex-shepherd's heart strings, but as king with judge's powers, David is also outraged at the sheer injustice of it. Then come those devastating words: 'You are that man!' and David is faced with his own lust and greed, deceit and disobedience. He has slept with another man's wife and had him killed in battle to cover her subsequent pregnancy. There are no excuses.

The death of the baby and the promise of family dysfunction seem a hard consequence of David's abuse of power. And yet, while he mourns, he does not accuse God of being unfair. At last, he is big enough and humble enough to blame only himself. In the mess that ensues, he desperately needs forgiveness and a restoration of his relationship with God whom he knows is a loving and merciful judge.

....

Is God highlighting attitudes in your life which are wrong? Thank him for loving you enough to want to make you more like him. Ask for his strength to be honest.

FB

Knowing God in heartbreak

[David] kept saying, 'My son Absalom! My son, my son Absalom! I wish I could have died instead of you! Absalom, my son, my son!'

'Home is where the hurt is' is a slogan we have used at our local Women's Aid centre for families fleeing domestic violence. It expresses the agonizing irony that the very place where we should feel safe and secure and loved may be where we are most wounded and damaged. While the refuge sees some of the more extreme cases, sadly, it is generally true for all of us that those closest to us are the ones who can hurt us most.

Somehow it all seems to go from bad to worse in David's family. Although family dysfunction and tragedy can never be put in a 'nut-shell', it involves lust and misery, hatred and revenge. When Ammon rapes his half-sister Tamar, inexcusably David, their father, does nothing to punish him. Tamar's furious brother Absalom eventually has Ammon killed. After three years in exile, Absalom is allowed home, but David refuses to see him. How different things might have turned out if only he had been courageous enough to talk over the painful issues with his hurting son! Instead, bitterness and hard-heartedness fester on both sides, until some eleven years after Tamar's rape, Absalom revolts against his father and declares himself king. David has to flee to the wilderness.

Despite poor parenting, David loves his children, and in the rock-bottom anguish of complete relationship collapse, his heart is softened and broken. A family feud becomes a national crisis, and while many thousands of troops are involved in the ensuing battle, he orders and begs, 'Be gentle with the young man Absalom for my sake' (NIV). After years of inclemency, he pleads for mercy for his erring son from his soldiers, and for himself from God. Tragically, there is no happy ending and Absalom is killed. It is too late for restoration.

....

Are you in a situation of family breakdown? Ask God to give you wisdom to know what you can change and what you must accept.

Read 2 Corinthians 1:3–5 for hope in your sorrow.

FB

Knowing God in dying

'Do what God tells you. Walk in the paths he shows you: Follow the life-map absolutely, keep an eye out for the signposts, his course for life set out in the revelation to Moses; then you'll get on well in whatever you do and wherever you go.'

This morning I heard that a dear 91-year-old friend just died. When I last saw her, we talked like we always have, but she looked shrunken physically, weary from pain and dependent on the decisions of family and doctors. Dying, at whatever age, is a horrible business.

It would be great to see David end his days in a blaze of glory. This passionate, generous man, described as 'a man after God's own heart' despite his failings, deserves to die in peace surrounded by loving family and friends. However, death often brings out the worst in people and the Bible does not shirk from telling us the truth. 1 Kings 1 and 2 recounts the sorry tale. David's servants see his dying as a problem: he cannot get warm, despite many blankets, and his vigour cannot even be aroused by the beautiful virgin Abishag who tends him. Adonijah, his eldest son, sees his dying as an opportunity to declare himself king. Bathsheba, encouraged by Nathan the prophet, sees his dying as a time to grasp both his fatherly and kingly responsibilities in the succession. For too long, he has let his children do what they want. They urge him to keep his promise and ensure that Solomon, Bathsheba's son, is crowned. Abishag, silent and lovely, seems to be the one person who gives without demand to this vulnerable man.

David's last words to Solomon, like his life, are a mixture of good and bad. He still holds on to some resentments, but he also recalls kindness. First and foremost, however, he impresses on his son the need to obey God. As king, he must never forget that he is also a man under authority. It is for this wholehearted lifelong devotion to his Sovereign Lord that David is remembered three thousand years later.

....

Like David, we will never be perfect in this life. Thank God that heaven is for sinners who have sought his forgiveness in Jesus, the Son of David.

Read Revelation 5 and join in the heavenly praise of the Lamb who has bought you with his blood.

FB

Have you noticed how contributors have pointed repeatedly to 1 Corinthians 13 over the last few weeks? Each of the writers was commissioned nearly two years ago. They were told the overall theme of these notes: 'Knowing God' and they were invited to contribute 14 notes on an aspect of that theme. They then drew on the inspiration God gives to those who ask and they completed their contributions more than a year ago. Love was not a particular focus of any of the aspects commissioned—yet the love that Paul describes has been referred to again and again.

As you approach these notes, what do you expect? Do you expect God to speak to you personally through the Bible and through what has been written?

The Bible is no ordinary book, as you will know if you have read some of its pages. Yes, it is a collection of 66 books of history, poetry, prophecy and letters to the first Christians (including how-to-be-church guidelines), but it is more than that. From Genesis to Revelation, these books and letters point to Jesus, who is described as 'word made flesh' (John 1:14). When Jesus was living in Israel he fleshed out the words in this amazing book. Before he went to the cross, he explained to the disciples that he would send the Holy Spirit: 'The Holy Spirit whom the Father will send at my request, will make everything plain to you. He will remind you of all the things I have told you' (John 14:26, THE MESSAGE).

Now that Jesus has risen from the dead and has returned to his Father in heaven, the Holy Spirit continues to bring the word of God to life. It is possible to read the Bible and find it meaningless. Paul explained this to the Corinthians in this chapter to which we have been pointed time and again in this series of notes: 'We don't yet see things clearly. We're squinting in a fog, peering through a mist. But it won't be long before the weather clears and the sun shines bright! We'll see it all then, see it all as clearly as God sees us, knowing him directly just as he knows us!' (1 Corinthians 13:12, THE MESSAGE).

What a prospect! To know God as he knows us! Meanwhile, if repetition means God wants to underline something from the Bible, then the repeated references to 1 Corinthians might mean God is speaking to you personally about his love for you and the type of love he is producing in you for others.

God in the Psalms

Your righteousness reaches to the skies, O God, you who have done great things. Who, O God, is like you? ... My lips will shout for joy when I sing praise to you—I, whom you have redeemed. My tongue will tell of your righteous acts.

Have you ever read someone else's love letters? Several years ago I was doing some historical research, and came across a collection of very old love letters in a dusty box, high on a shelf in the archives. The affection and trust that the woman had had for her fiancé still shone in the pages.

The Psalms remind me of love letters. They are the timeless hymns of love that ancient Israel offered to God. They are collected into five books (Psalms 1—41; 42—72; 73—89; 90-106; 107—150) and were written over a period of about 600 years. They begin with David about 950BC (whose name appears beside 73 of them) and reflect every aspect of the relationship between Israel and their God. There is love, sorrow, anger, repentance, trust and thanksgiving.

A very clear picture of God emerges in the Psalms. This was the God of King David and ancient Israel, and this is the same God whom we Christians worship today. If you want to get to know God better, you can hardly do better than to read the Psalms.

The first, most fundamental thing about God that comes through in the Psalms is that there *is* a God, and that there is only *one* God. Theologians call this belief monotheism. Many people today would call it nonsense. Atheists say there is no god at all. Psalm 14:1 observes, 'The fool says in his heart, "There is no God."' The Psalms do not try to prove God's existence; it is seen as so obvious as not to need 'proving'.

Some may say that we have no right to say that our God is the only true God. Again, Psalm 96:5 says simply: 'For all the gods of the nations are idols, but the Lord made the heavens.' It is a case of take him or leave him.

....

'Know that the Lord is God. It is he who made us… we are his people, the sheep of his pasture' (Psalm 100:3).

Read Psalms 29, 47, 96 and 100 for a glorious picture of the one and only true God.

AC

Glorious majesty

The heavens declare the glory of God; the skies proclaim the work of his hands. Day after day they pour forth speech; night after night they display knowledge.

Did you ever see the film *Shirley Valentine*? There is a scene where Shirley is in Greece, watching the sun set over the Aegean Sea and the mountains beyond. It is a glorious sunset—the sun blazing gold in a sky shot full of purples and fiery reds. The majesty, the glory, the eternal peace of the beauty of it all affects Shirley deeply. She realizes at that moment that her old constricted life in Manchester is emotionally and spiritually starved: she 'falls in love with love' at that moment, as she says.

Shirley felt the presence of 'a love beyond' at that moment. The Psalms could have told her what—or who—that 'love' was. Shirley was sensing the God who had made the sunset.

The Psalms are full of the majesty, the glory, the power of God. It's incredible how we can 'downsize' the God of the universe into the pleasant but faintly boring God who lives in church on Sunday mornings—sung about in squeaky-pitched hymns, yawned about during the sermon. For a dose of the real God, just go outside instead and look at a sunset, or the stars at night, and remember who made them.

God must look down on us in sheer amazement at times—how can we find him dull or far away? He is putting on a spectacular *Son et Lumiere* for us every day and every night. He is keeping nature running. He knows each one of us before we are even born. His power and goodness are evident everywhere.

Read Psalm 104 for a vivid description of God's majesty at work in the world. 'Who can proclaim the mighty acts of the Lord, or fully declare his praise?' (Psalm 106:2).

....

Lord, help me to see your majesty, to recognize your all-powerful presence in the world.

Psalm 145 offers further insights into God's greatness.

AC

Holy, holy, holy

Great is the Lord… he is exalted over all the nations. Let them praise your great and awesome name—he is holy… worship at his foot-stool, he is holy… worship at his holy mountain, for the Lord our God is holy.

In South Africa, several years ago, I visited a Hindu temple where I saw a tired young mother walking around some stones on an altar. They represented the gods that ruled the planets, and she had been told that she had to walk around this altar 100 times in order to placate the gods or they might kill her infant son. The young mother had no doubt that the gods were powerful, but it never occurred to her to consider them good.

Yet the one true God is not only almighty—he is *good*. His goodness is so high above ours, so pure and without stain, that we call him *holy*. The *Concise Oxford Dictionary*'s definition of holy includes: 'sacred; morally and spiritually perfect'. God is morally perfect? This would have been a surprise to many people in the ancient Near East, as it would do to millions of non-Christian people today. 'God' is always associated with power, but not necessarily with goodness.

In Baal worship in Old Testament times, worshippers heated a statue of the god to red hot, and then placed a live baby in its fiery arms to be roasted alive. This was what their god demanded. But the true God is not a raging, petulant power who has to be placated. He does not have evil designs on us. He does not require our suffering or our deaths to be satisfied. Instead, our God is *holy*; utterly perfect; the source of all goodness, all purity, all kindness; without shadow of evil or malice or cruelty.

We approach such divine goodness with awe and worship. We pour out our hearts in thanksgiving that such a holy God is indeed the ultimate ruler of the universe. The holiness of God is a reassurance to us. 'God's in his heaven, all's right with the world', as a poet once said.

Imagine for a moment what life would be like if God were not good. If the ultimate power in the universe was, in fact, evil.

Read Psalm 103 to see God's holiness overflowing in action: his ongoing goodness, love and compassion towards us.

AC

Created by hand—with care

He set the earth on its foundations... makes springs pour water... makes grass grow for the cattle, and plants for people to cultivate... the earth is full of your creatures. There is the sea, vast and spacious, teeming with creatures beyond number... [All creatures] look to you... may the Lord rejoice in his works.

Each summer when I go to Cornwall, I enjoy browsing in those up-market tourist shops in Padstow and St Ives and Fowey. Many items for sale—jumpers, biscuits, even crisps—boast that they are 'hand-crafted'. The implication, of course, is that when an individual person has been involved in the production, the end product will come out much better, and be more valuable.

It amuses me to think that we want our biscuits and jumpers to have been 'hand-crafted' by somebody, but when it comes to our planet, and our very selves, millions of us are content to think we are the end result of a sort of an indifferent cosmic machine-made effort!

The Psalms have no room for evolution. There is not a single verse anywhere that even hints that the world and ourselves happened by chance, over time. Time and again we read that God *created*, that he 'hand-crafted' not just the world, but each one of us as well.

Psalm 139 is God's way of telling us that each one of us is indeed 'hand-crafted': 'For you created my inmost being; you knit me together in my mother's womb... I am fearfully and wonderfully made; your works are wonderful.' The psalmist urges all creation to praise God for this very reason: 'for he commanded, and they were *created*' (Psalm 148:5). 'When you send your Spirit, they are *created*' (Psalm 104:30).

Some 'posh' merchandise comes with a lifelong cover or guarantee. God is like that, say the Psalms. Psalm 121 promises us excellent ongoing guarantee cover: 'The Lord will watch over your coming and going, both now and for evermore.'

....

How does the realization that God knows even the number of hairs on your head affect your feelings of self-worth?

Read the whole of Psalm 139 to discover how intimately God knows each one of us.

AC

Your love endures for ever

I will sing of the Lord's great love for ever; with my mouth I will make your faithfulness known through all generations. I will declare that your love stands firm for ever, that you established your faithfulness in heaven itself.

When I was 16, I had my first boyfriend. He was away at school, and so we wrote each other letters. The word 'love' was used in various capital letters about a hundred times a letter. Love, love, love, love, *love*! Thirty-five years on, I still remember the glow that transfused me when I read those words. This guy loved *me*! Wow! It lasted about three months, when we realized we didn't even much like each other, but hey, it was great while it lasted.

The Psalms are love letters between God and us. And this love doesn't die in three months. Listen to this: 'Give thanks to the Lord, for he is good. His love endures for ever' (Psalm 136:1).

'His love endures for ever' is a refrain that runs 26 times in Psalm 136 alone! And so it goes on: love, love, love, love, love!

'The earth is *full* of his unfailing love' (33:5). 'How *priceless* is your unfailing love!' (36:7). 'God *sends* his love and his faithfulness' (57:3). 'In the morning *I will sing* of your love' (59:16). 'Your love *is better than life*' (63:3). 'Love and faithfulness *go before you*' (89:14). 'Your love, O Lord, *supported me*' (94:18). 'The Lord… is slow to anger, *abounding* in love' (103:8). 'The Lord's love *is with those* who fear him' (103:17). God's love for us is mentioned 118 times in the Psalms—just in case we didn't get the point the first 117 times!

Our God is not a faraway God. He wants to be near you, to care for you, to nurture you. 'He will *never* leave you or forsake you. Do *not* be afraid, do *not* be discouraged' (Deuteronomy 31:8). You are not alone, and you are not worthless. You are beloved and precious to God.

....

Love becomes obvious over time in a relationship. Why not aim to spend at least ten minutes every day for the next week reading a psalm? Give God a chance to speak to you about his love for you. He is there, but perhaps you need to hear him more clearly.

AC

Our redeemer

Have mercy on me, O God, according to your unfailing love… blot out my transgressions. Wash away all my iniquity and cleanse me from my sin… Create in me a pure heart, O God, and renew a steadfast spirit within me… Restore to me the joy of your salvation.

In July 1967 my family were still living in New York, and I was sent to summer camp, as children are in the States. This one was a Christian camp in Ontario. I was 12 years old and, though not a mass murderer or anything obviously 'wicked', I arrived at the camp with a dead, sullen, angry, dark spirit. My family were Christian, and I believed in God, but he meant little to me personally.

Four days later, after one of the evening meetings that the camp leaders held, we were invited to go forward to pray, if we wanted 'to get to know God better'. I went forward, and prayed, and an hour later had the most profound religious experience of my life. I would have said I was a Christian before that night, but that night I felt my spirit reborn, and God's redemptive love towered over and around and beneath me. I have never before or since felt anything so intense, but since that night I have never for a moment doubted that Jesus Christ has redeemed me.

Redemption is your first personal experience of God, no matter how much you may have thought about him or feel you know about him. It was through redemption that the Israelites first encountered Yahweh. At the time, they were wretched slaves in Egypt. Then Moses came along and told them that God had chosen them to be his people and that he was going to rescue them. The rescue began with the Passover meal, and continued with a march out of Egypt and an unexpected crossing of the Red Sea on foot. Their redemption had begun.

The Psalms often look back to this act of national redemption, but Psalm 34:22 also speaks of personal redemption: 'The Lord redeems his servants; no one will be condemned who takes refuge in him.'

....

How would you describe your first personal experience of God?

Read Psalm 103 for a glorious full-colour picture of what God's redemption can mean for you.

AC

Follow the maker's instructions

I have chosen the way of truth; I have set my heart on your laws.
I hold fast to your statutes, O Lord; do not let me be put to shame.
I run in the path of your commands, for you have set my heart free.

Do you have a life coach? They are those expensive experts who come alongside you and make sure that you develop all the 'life skills' to make the most of your life—your work, your leisure, your family. It's about knowing how to make your life succeed, living so as to capitalize on your best traits, and minimize your weaknesses. Life coaches can cost a fortune, but some celebrities, at least, think they are worth it.

The Psalms make clear that ancient Israel had a life coach—Jehovah. When he brought them out of the land of Egypt, they were a rag-tag bunch of slaves with no idea of how to act before God, or in supportive community with each other. They had no code of conduct beyond mere struggle for personal survival.

And so God, having redeemed them, gave them the law. It spelled out in clear detail how they were to run their lives—before God, within their communities and in their families. Obedience to the law would mean that their nation would flourish. Rebellion would disrupt their relationship with God and tear the social fabric of their society.

The Psalms are full of praise for God's law. His 'precepts' are good. God's law is never seen as restrictive, but as liberating. 'The law of the Lord is perfect, reviving the soul,' declares the psalmist (Psalm 19.7). God's law protects us: 'The law of his God is in his heart; his feet do not slip' (Psalm 37:31).

Of course, we all fail and sin. So I find the last verse of Psalm 119 especially comforting. After 175 verses of saying how much he loved God's commands, the psalmist suddenly blurts out in verse 176: 'I have *strayed like a lost sheep*. Seek your servant, for I have not forgotten your commands.'

....

It is fashionable today to mock anyone who mentions the Ten
Commandments. But since when did murder, lying, adultery
and slander bring anyone great happiness? God's law brings life,
not death.

AC

God our judge

Rise up, O Judge of the earth… Does he who implanted the ear not hear? Does he who formed the eye not see? Does he who disciplines nations not punish? Does he who teaches human beings lack knowledge? … Blessed are those you discipline, O Lord, those you teach from your law.

There is a downside to having a loving creator God who knows you intimately and gives you guidance on how to live your life. The downside is that under these circumstances it is very difficult to sin and to get away with it. In fact, you don't get away with it. Before you sin, you can think of all the arguments as to why you should go ahead and do this thing. After you sin, the discomfort and guilt begin… you feel embarrassed before God, and distant from him, and if you don't repent and put it right immediately, things only go from bad to worse.

The psalms are full of this aspect of God's dealings with us. This is because the Israelites had lots and lots of experience of rebelling against God… and so lots and lots of judgment.

Of course judgment is not just national—it is personal. Whenever we sin, we come under God's righteous judgment. The psalmist knew it all too well: 'O Lord, do not rebuke me in your anger… For your arrows have pierced me, and your hand has come down upon me… my bones have no soundness because of my sin. My guilt has overwhelmed me.' You would think that at this point the psalmist would be doing his best to put as much space between himself and God as was possible. But no, for the Psalm continues: 'O Lord *do not forsake* me; be *not* far from me, O my God. *Come quickly to help me*, O Lord my Saviour.'

Psalm 37:27 gives this simple but excellent advice: 'Turn from evil and do good; then you will dwell in the land for ever.' Psalm 130:3–4 observes: 'If you, O Lord, kept a record of sins, O Lord, who could stand? But with you *there is forgiveness*; therefore you are feared.

....

Have you done something that is troubling you? Don't let it drag on—take it to God now. He promises 'If we confess our sins, he is faithful and just and will forgive us our sins and purify us from all unrighteousness' (1 John 1:9).

AC

The good shepherd

The Lord is my shepherd, I shall not be in want. He makes me lie down in green pastures, he leads me beside quiet waters, he restores my soul. He guides me in the path of righteousness for his name's sake. Even though I walk through the valley of the shadow of death, I will fear no evil.

Many years ago the *Reader's Digest* (July 1950) ran an interview with an old Basque shepherd named Fernando D'Alfonso. He had some illuminating observations to make on the 23rd psalm.

The Lord is my shepherd; I shall not be in want: 'Sheep trust their shepherd to provide grazing,' explained D'Alfonso. 'It may be that he will take them back over the same hills; it may be that he will go on to new grazing ground. They do not worry.'

He makes me lie down in green pastures: Sheep graze from about 3.30am until about ten. Then they lie down to chew the cud for several hours, and rest. And so the good shepherd leads his flock to a shady fine place by midday, because 'sheep resting in such happy surroundings feel contentment'.

He leads me beside quiet waters: Sheep are frightened of gurgling water, so the shepherd finds a rock pool, or else digs one with his own hands. The good shepherd knows our weaknesses.

Even though I walk through the valley of the shadow of death, I will fear no evil… your rod and your staff, they comfort me: The actual Valley of the Shadow of Death is south of the Jericho road, leading to the Dead Sea. It is a four and a half mile narrow defile through a high mountain range, with deep gullies, which the sheep must jump. Some don't make it, and then the shepherd uses his staff to haul them to safety. Should wild dogs attack, the staff becomes a rod to defend the sheep. 'Thus the sheep have learnt to fear no evil even in the Valley of the Shadow of Death, for their master is there to protect them from harm.'

When have you sensed that the Good Shepherd was leading you, providing for you and shielding you from danger?

Read Psalm 25 for an assurance of the Good Shepherd's daily love and care for us.

AC

Goodness and mercy

You prepare a table before me in the presence of my enemies. You anoint my head with oil; my cup overflows. Surely goodness and love will follow me all the days of my life, and I will dwell in the house of the Lord for ever.

I have always loved the 23rd psalm, but I have not always understood it. Thus I was helped by the *Reader's Digest* article I mentioned yesterday, where Fernando D'Alfonso shared his observations. Although Jesus is not, of course, mentioned by name in the Psalms, this is a shining portrait of him, our Good Shepherd.

You prepare a table before me in the presence of my enemies: Grazing in the Holy Land can be treacherous. So the shepherd grubs out every poisonous weed he can see. He then stacks the poisonous plants on little stone pyres, some of which date from Old Testament times. By the following day they are dry enough to burn. Only then, 'when the pasture is free from poisonous plants, the sheep are led into it and, in the presence of their plant enemies, they eat in peace'.

You anoint my head with oil; my cup overflows: Beside every sheepfold there is a big earthen bowl of olive oil and a large jar of water. As the sheep are brought into the fold at night, the shepherd examines each one for briers, thorns or scratches. Any wounds are cleaned and anointed with oil. Then the shepherd dips a large cup into the pottery jar and brings it out for the sheep to drink. It is never half full, but always overflowing. When all the sheep are at rest, the shepherd settles down with his staff, wraps himself in his woollen robe, and lies across the gateway, becoming the door of the sheepfold. He will stays there all night, guarding his sheep.

Surely goodness and love will follow me all the days of my life: If human shepherds take this care of sheep, our good shepherd will certainly not do less for us.

....

Have you ever felt divine protection in the presence of your enemies?

Read Psalm 55 for comfort in times of trouble.

AC

When God is silent

How long, O Lord? Will you forget me for ever? How long will you hide your face from me? How long must I wrestle with my thoughts and every day have sorrow in my heart? How long will my enemy triumph over me? Look on me and answer, O Lord my God.

There are times in life when heaven's door seems shut. God is silent. You pray, but there is no sense of the presence of God, and your troubles are mounting on every side. Christians throughout the centuries have known these times as 'the dark night of the soul', 'the wilderness experience', 'times of testing'.

The Psalms accept that our experience of God may include these silent times. I find Psalm 88 to be the darkest of all the psalms: 'My soul is full of trouble... I cry to you for help, O Lord; in the morning my prayer comes before you. *Why, O Lord, do you reject me and hide your face from me?* You have taken my companions and my loved ones from me; the darkness is my closest friend.'

When a personal tragedy hit me several years ago, I felt utterly alone. Those on whom I had counted had left me. Even God seemed distant. But as the months went by, I began to realize that just because I didn't *feel* his presence, it did not mean God was not there.

Then I could say with the psalmist: 'When my heart was grieved and my spirit embittered, I was senseless and ignorant... Yet I am *always* with you; you *hold me by my right hand*... my flesh and my heart may fail, but God *is* the strength of my heart and *my portion for ever*' (Psalm 73:21, 23, 26). In practice, I found that God's silence actually helped me grow in faith. Like the psalmist who did not really understand God's silence either, we can simply conclude: 'But I trust in your unfailing love; my heart rejoices in your salvation. I will sing to the Lord, for he has been good to me.'

Faith is faith in a person, not our feelings at any given time.

....

Take time today to notice God's presence in your life, in all the different circumstances. End the day thanking God.

Read Hebrews 11 for a magnificent listing of those who honoured God by their faith, even when they could not see him.

AC

Our faithful God

Hear O Lord, and answer me, for I am poor and needy. Guard my life, for I am devoted to you. You are my God; save your servant who trusts in you. Have mercy on me, O Lord, for I call to you all day long... But you, O Lord, are a compassionate and gracious God, slow to anger, abounding in love and faithfulness.

A friend of mine got divorced. Her husband had been on a fling that had lasted most of their marriage. She had lost count of all his various lady friends. She had learned the hard way the sad truth of the song from the musical *Chess*: 'Nobody's on *nobody's* side... never let a friend fool you twice'.

Another friend of mine married an engineer. She admitted that his constant enthusiasm for obscure bits of big engines made conversation a bit dull. 'But I can depend on him,' she said. 'He is totally faithful.'

Have you ever been betrayed? Lied to? Cheated on? If so, you will know the feeling of the ground opening beneath your feet—when someone you have trusted as a friend turns out to be actually a bit of an enemy. The Psalms assure us time and again that God is *faithful*. He will not let you down. He will not desert you. 'Trust in him at all times, O people; pour out your hearts to him' (Psalm 62:8). Over the centuries millions of Christians have done just this, and can echo the words of the psalmist: 'The Lord is faithful to all his promises and loving towards all he has made' (Psalm 145:13). 'God sends his love and faithfulness' (Psalm 57:3).

The psalms warn us that God is more dependable than the most powerful people: 'when their spirit departs, they return to ground; on that very day their plans come to nothing. Blessed is he whose help is the God of Jacob... who remains faithful for ever.' The reason for God's great faithfulness is in his personal love for us: 'Your love, O Lord, reaches to the heavens, your faithfulness to the skies' (Psalm 36:5).

What is your response to God's faithfulness?

See Psalm 85 to be assured—again—of God's love and faithfulness towards us.

AC

Rock of ages

In you, O Lord, I have taken refuge; let me never be put to shame; deliver me in your righteousness. Turn your ear to me, come quickly to my rescue; be my rock of refuge, a strong fortress to save me. Since you are my rock and my fortress, for the sake of your name lead and guide me.

God is my rock; my stronghold. Those words never meant much to me until I visited an island off the far north of Scotland, and crawled out to the edge of a cliff to look over the sea birds nesting in their hundreds on the side of the cliff below. I wouldn't recommend this as a way of doing Bible exegesis, because the height gave me vertigo, and the wind nearly blew my head off, but ever since that afternoon I've understood what it means to have God as your rock.

Those birds were thousands of feet up, and the wind and the weather would be fearsome at times (it was bad enough on a sunny afternoon). Yet they seemed oblivious to the elements beating against them. Why? Because the elements were not touching them. All the fury of the wind was beating on the rock. Those sea birds were sheltered in little crevices of the rock, and the rock was taking all the beating of the wind. As long as those little frail birds just stayed close to the rock, they were fine.

Of course, the psalmist himself had hands-on experience of hiding in rocks. There were no castles in those days to hide in, and so in the wilderness, he would have sought refuge from his enemies by hiding out in the crevices of some great rock in the wilderness. It would protect him from the heat of the sun, the wind, any rain, and keep him out of sight of his enemies. The elements that would have destroyed him fell harmlessly on the rock, which was well equipped to take them.

The psalmist wrote: 'He who dwells in the shelter of the Most High *will rest in the shadow* of the Almighty' (Psalm 91:1–2).

In times of trouble, God longs for us to take shelter in him. He never intended that you should face any storm in life all alone.

Read Psalm 91 for a beautiful description of God's protection over us.

AC

Joy to the Lord!

Praise the Lord from the heavens... all his angels... all his heavenly hosts... sun and moon... shining stars... from the earth... great sea creatures... lightning and hail, snow and clouds, stormy winds... mountains... fruit trees and all cedars, wild animals and all cattle, small creatures and flying birds, kings of the earth and all nations.

Have you ever been to Last Night at the Proms? Near the end of the evening the conductor brings in every instrument going, and then the choir, and then he turns to the audience to bring them in as well. People are even jumping up and down *outside* the building... Well, as the fifth book of the Psalms draws to a close, it's 'Last Night of the Psalms' time; for this psalm, and several others, simply *resound* with overwhelming exuberance and excitement. They are brimming with such joy and praise that they want everything in all creation to join in on the act. Everybody together now: Praise the Lord!

So the last major thing about God that I find in the Psalms is that our God is *praiseworthy*. The word 'praise' is found in nearly every one of the 150 psalms. It is our only possible response to an almighty eternal loving creator who has made the heavens and the earth, who knows us as we are, but still loves us, forgives us, redeems us, and protects us from evil. No wonder the psalmist urges: 'Let Israel *rejoice* in their Maker; let the people of Zion be *glad* in their King. Let them *praise* his name with dancing and make music to him with tambourine and harp. For the Lord takes delight in his people... Let the saints *rejoice* in this honour and *sing* for joy on their beds' (Psalm 149:2–5).

These magnificent psalms of praise give us a hint of what eternity will be like. Resounding with joy and love: between God and all his creation. The sheer happiness, comradeship and exultation of Last Night of the Proms gives us the merest echo of what it will be like when one day we join the heavenly host to sing praises to our wonderful God.

....

Praising God, thanking him for just being there for us, is the best way to restore a true sense of perspective on life.

Read Psalms 144—150 for the grand finale of the psalms. It is deafening in its joyous thanksgiving!

AC

Although Anne Coomes and Alie Stibbe have both been invited to focus our attention on the Psalms, over the next fortnight you will notice how different their thoughts are about the same Bible book. Anne has focused on the psalms as love letters, revealing different aspects of God's character to us. Over the next two weeks, Alie Stibbe will be helping us to live in God's presence, even when he doesn't feel close. Although they have worked from the same Bible material, God has given them very different ways in which to understand his word.

With most books, I read them once, and never return to them. It's the same with most films: I rarely want to go back to a story, when I already know the ending. The Bible is quite different. It can be read again and again, and never fails to offer fresh insights, because it is more than simply words on a page. The written words are the raw material for the Holy Spirit to write God's love letter into our hearts and to guide us as we seek to live our lives God's way.

Of course we can get it wrong, hence the need to be part of a church where the Bible is valued. As we remain accountable to God and to each other, we can avoid misguided interpretations. And, of course, there are parts of the Bible which are difficult to understand and which cause controversy, but that's not the case with most of it.

Because the Holy Spirit wants us to know God, it is possible to return to the same passage of scripture again and again, gaining fresh insights with every reading.

My great uncle lived in Australia where he ran a bakery. His working day started early, but he got up even earlier than work demanded, so he could read his Bible. Once in retirement, the pattern continued, and I remember him visiting us in England and waking to hear him already reading the Bible aloud to my great aunt. He never tired of reading God's word, although he must have read it through many times.

As you continue to read through the Psalms, expect God to speak to you individually and in a way that is uniquely relevant to your circumstances. Like any loving parent, God wants to speak to you, his child.

Mountain tops and valleys

Do not hide your face from your servant; answer me quickly, for I am in trouble. Come near and rescue me... because of my foes.

There are times when God feels very far away; life becomes overwhelming and we begin to sink under all the demands made on us by circumstances. This has been my recent experience—to the extent that I felt I had nothing to share with you. As I pounded on heaven's door, I met the Lord in the pages of C.S. Lewis' *The Silver Chair* during my son's bedtime story. Aslan the lion was talking to Jill Pole in the 'Wood Between the Worlds' high above Narnia: he assigned her with a task and charged her to memorize four signs that would help her along the way. She was told it is easy to remember the signs on the mountain top, because the air was clear and the lion was there to prompt you. But in the valley the air would be thicker, thoughts are distorted, and it would be easy to forget the signs and miss the way. This hit me like a punch in the face—yes, I had met the Lord on the mountain top, he had made the task clear and given me my 'signs'. But now I was in the valley, in the thick of the fight, and had been for a while. I had allowed my thoughts to become distorted, missed the way and lost any sense of God's presence. How easy it is to let that happen—yet how close God is when we come to our senses and turn to look for him!

Perhaps you feel you've lost the way and the mountain top is far behind? Let's remind ourselves of four signs God has given us in the Psalms to help us keep close to him in the valley of everyday life: promises about commission, companionship, compulsion and completion.

....

God is closer than you think. Are you standing with your back to the throne? Let him gently turn you round and gather you into his embrace.

Read Psalm 130. Feeling bereft of God's presence gives birth to longing in our soul.

AS

Commission 1: Chosen

For you created my inmost being; you knit me together in my mother's womb… All the days ordained for me were written in your book before one of them came to be.

After my encounter with Aslan's words to Jill I began mulling over what the signs were that the Lord had given me concerning the particular task I am struggling with in the thick air of my own valley. At the moment I am coming towards the end of my first academic year as a full-time research student. With four children and a husband leading a large church through major transition, this has been more of a challenge than I realized. Doubts began to surface. Did I hear the Lord right? Am I really up to this? Is this just a major mid-life crisis? What's it all for? It was time to sit down, think back to when I was 'on the mountain' last summer and try to remember 'the signs'.

Eventually I remembered the first sign was 'commission'—the fact we are chosen, called and cherished by the Lord. He lovingly designed each of us with a specific task in mind that only we can fulfil. Our 'chosen-ness' is expressed in the most amazing way in Psalm 139. When I read verse 13 it reminds me that I am made just the way God wanted—physically, mentally and emotionally—for a reason that unfolds little by little if I live faithfully every day that I am given. There is no point wanting long black hair, an extravert personality, to dumb down a bit or live to be 100, because my physical attributes, reflective nature and capacity to think deeply and analytically, and the length of my life, were given to me with good reason—even if I can't see the sum of that reason. This is no excuse not to change and grow, but a reason to do the best with what we have been given every moment that we have it.

....

Thank God that he has chosen and called you. You are cherished by him.

Read Isaiah 49 and consider: you are chosen by God according to his special purpose, however small you may feel.

AS

Commission 2: Called

The Lord is near to all who call on him, to all who call on him in truth. He fulfils the desires of those who fear him; he hears their cry and saves them.

In one sense every human being is 'chosen' by God in that he designed them and planned the life he hoped they would lead. Unfortunately, not everybody comes to know the abundant life that 'fulfils all their desires'. A person needs to respond when they hear the Lord calling them, and choose that life for themselves (Hebrews 3:8).

If you are reading this, you have probably heard God's call and made that choice. But there are further calls to hear and choices to be made—the Christian life is a moment-by-moment choice to answer the call to put Jesus first, and has moments when we hear a call to particular tasks for which we are the best candidate. Yet we often get things the wrong way round. In the struggles we face we think we are the ones doing the calling—but are we?

Back to *The Silver Chair*: Jill and Eustace are trying to escape the school bullies. They call on the name of Aslan. To Jill it is a game, but she finds herself on the mountain top with the amazing lion. During their conversation it is clear Jill thinks she initiated the action, but Aslan says, 'You wouldn't have called me, unless I had been calling you first!'

The Lord is near to those who call on him, because he is already calling them with a future and a hope in mind. He rescues them out of their difficulties, not to sit by still waters (not for long anyway), but to respond to a new challenge that will fulfil the desires of their heart. When that challenge gets difficult, then it's time to remember the sign: 'You didn't choose me, but I chose you and appointed you to go and bear fruit—fruit that will last' (John 15:16).

....

What special task the Lord has entrusted you with for now? Ask the Lord to remind you of how he called you to that task and strengthen you.

Read Psalm 139:7–12 and know that when you call him, he is already calling you.

AS

Commission 3: Cherished

Many, O Lord my God, are the wonders you have done. The things you planned for us no one can recount to you; were I to speak of them, they would be too many to declare.

The thing about the Lord having given each of us a commission—calling and choosing us—is not only the sense of purpose that he gives to our lives and the fulfilment that brings with it, but also the fact that it is a good purpose. When things get difficult, it is always good to remember that part of being 'chosen' and 'called' is that we are also 'cherished'. If you cherish something, you hold it dear, you nurture it tenderly so that it grows to meet its full potential. That is what the Lord intends for us as part of our commission, and it is wonderfully summed up in Jeremiah 29:11: 'I know the plans I have for you,' declares the Lord, 'plans to prosper you and not to harm you, plans to give you a hope and a future.'

When, like Jill, we're down in the valley where the air is thick and we can't think straight, we tend to forget that the Lord's plan for us is a good one, one that he called us into in order to fulfil our potential and pave the way for the future—all for his glory, mind you, not ours! We let things get out of perspective and, like the psalmist in today's reading, we find that life becomes a slimy pit full of mud and mire in which we can't get a firm footing. That is the time to stop struggling—struggling in a mire only makes you sink deeper. Stop and call on the Lord—he will set your feet back on firm ground if you stand still long enough for him to remind you of the wonders he has already done in your life (v. 5a) and the promises he has made to you concerning your present and your future (v. 5b).

....

Lord, thank you that I am the apple of your eye; when life gets difficult, hide me in the shadow of your wings and restore your perspective in my heart and mind (Psalm 17:8–9).

AS

Companionship 1: Presence

Where can I go from your Spirit? Where can I flee from your presence? If I go up to the heavens, you are there; if I make my bed in the depths, you are there.

We have been looking at the first of four signs that we have to remember when the going gets tough and we lose the sense of God's presence: commission. Commission is basically about being chosen and called according to the Lord's good purpose to do a specific task. The second sign that we need to remember is companionship—not only are we sent by the Lord, but he actually goes with us. Even if we think we don't see him some of the time, he turns up in the most unlikely places—the words of a song, a chance meeting with a stranger, a prompt in our heart.

Back on the mountain top in *The Silver Chair*, Aslan the Lion has commissioned Jane; then he carries her on his breath across land and sea to Narnia where the adventure takes place. She thinks he is behind her on the mountain, but the lion keeps appearing throughout the adventure so that you get the impression he has been there ahead of time to plan the way and direct her even when the landscape is desolate and the circumstances dire.

God's Holy Spirit is described in the Bible as 'breath' (*ruach*); when we are sent out on our chosen task, we are carried on that Spirit wherever we go, and that Spirit is God's presence with us. We can never get away from him—look at today's verse—even if we travel to the moon or go on a diving expedition to the bottom of the Mariana Trench! If the Lord is present in such extremes, he is certainly present in our everyday emotional extremes in the commonplace. We often miss his presence because we are too busy to stop and listen, or too wrapped up in our own self-pity to look upwards rather than inwards.

....

Lord, thank you that your hand holds me fast whatever the circumstances. May I never be too self-absorbed to know your Spirit's presence.

Read Psalm 42. Remember the mountain top, connect with him in your heart and know that he is the Lord of your life.

AS

Companionship 2: Provision

Fear the Lord, you his saints [chosen ones], for those who fear him lack nothing. The lions may grow weak and hungry, but those who seek the Lord lack no good thing.

I confess I struggle with worry about material provision—not that I want to be rich, mind you—but I get concerned about providing the necessities for a family of six in the present, and fret over what will happen to us as a couple when we are eventually 'put out to grass'. A clergy stipend doesn't go very far with a house full of teenagers, and as my husband works all the hours God sends, anyway, I tend to feel it is down to me to find the necessary extras.

That can be an intolerable burden, especially when my Protestant work ethic gets out of hand and I collapse in a wobbling, completely good-for-nothing, migraine-ridden heap. Then I realize I have forgotten a vital aspect of the second sign—the fact that the Lord provides all we need every step of the way, including time to stop and rest. Today I have had to stop and remind myself that I sought the Lord over being a full-time student, that provision of Research Council funding was the confirmation to go ahead, because that would cover some unexpected expenses that would be incurred by one child over the next four years. OK, so I had to turn down a very exciting publishing project today, but I am called to do what I am doing, even though today every fibre is screaming 'I want out!'

Practising God's presence in the everyday means aligning our focus with his; doing what we are called to do because we are called, not because of material gain. He has provided all we need for now and will deliver the rest if we put him first. That takes the stress out of the everyday and helps us to get on with the job in hand.

Forget not his benefits! Taking time to list at least three blessings in a notebook every night has been proven to make life healthier. When did you last count yours?

AS

Companionship 3: Protection

My help comes from the Lord… He will not let your foot slip—he who watches over you will not slumber… [he] will keep you from all harm—he will watch over your life.

Back to *The Silver Chair*! On her quest through the northern lands with her two companions, Jill forgot the signs. She allowed herself to become distracted by the thought of material comfort when the going got tough and, even though they literally fell into one of the signs, they didn't realize it because they had lost their focus and ended up in mortal danger. Thankfully, circumstances conspired to save them and put them back on the right track.

When things go wrong and we miss the way, putting ourselves and others in actual or spiritual danger, the Lord always has 'Plan B' waiting up his sleeve for the moment we come to our senses. And in retrospect, 'Plan B' has a strange habit of turning out to have been 'Plan A' all along—but only when the key factor of acknowledging our fault is put into the equation.

One of my lifelong key verses has been Proverbs 3:6: 'In all your ways acknowledge the Lord and he shall direct your paths' (NKJV). I have always wanted the Lord's 'Plan A' for my life, but I am very human. 'Down in the valley where the air is thick' I do forget the signs, get distracted and make life difficult for myself and those around me. However, I am convinced that, because I have an underlying desire to follow God's preordained path, when I get things wrong and eventually confess it, I find that it was all part of the plan and that I was marvellously protected from a hundred and one things that could have gone worse during the course of my detour. The Lord's companionship is not just a 'fuzzy feeling', but practical—he provides and protects along the way if we are set on living according to his purposes.

....

Thank you, Lord, that you watch over me now and for ever, that you are my help, my strength and my protection.

Read Isaiah 30:19–21, and listen to the voice behind you. See the right way and walk in it.

AS

Compulsion 1: Rock

From the ends of the earth I call to you, I call as my heart grows faint; lead me to a rock that is higher than I.

Thinking about four signs that help us to practise God's presence when the going gets difficult I not only realized that we need to remember our commission and the Lord's companionship, but also that the Lord is the one who keeps us going when the going gets tough—he is the one who compels us.

The other Sunday I sat in a sunny patch on the sofa and caught the beginning of the women's race in the London marathon and ended up watching Paula Radcliffe run until she finished. At one stage she stopped with cramp, but got up and started again at the same fast pace—there was something that compelled her to keep going. The commentator kept telling us Paula wanted to beat her record—that would have compelled her, but as I thought about it later, what probably helped keep her going were her pacemakers, the crowds who were rooting for her along the way and knowing her husband was waiting for her at the finishing line.

Marathon running is a very obvious metaphor not only for life itself, but for any task that needs sustained physical effort, mental determination and perseverance. Doing research feels like that sometimes, as can caring for a disabled relative, facing a serious illness or a financial crisis. When we're in anything for the long haul our hearts can grow faint. That is the time when we especially need to call out to the Lord, from what can seem like the ends of the earth, asking him to 'lead us to a rock higher than ourselves'—in other words, to be our strength and song; the one who compels us when we feel like quitting; the one who sets the pace, cheers us on and waits at the finishing line with arms open wide.

Thank you, Lord, that your strength is enough for the task you've called me to. Help me to know your pace and to keep it until I reach the finishing line.

Read Hebrews 12:1–3. Is there anything you need to 'strip off' to run more effectively?

AS

Compulsion 2: Rod

Even though I walk through the valley of the shadow of death, I will fear no evil, for you are with me; your rod and your staff, they comfort me.

I have just had a busy fortnight; everything needed doing or finishing at once—and life seemed to close in on me. When the going gets tough like this, I remember 'valley of the shadow of death' in Psalm 23. This is not because my deadlines are going to kill me, though it can feel that way, but because this valley was the kind known to the psalmist from his shepherding days. Occasionally he would have led his sheep through long narrow ravines in which the sheep would have lost sight of the shepherd up-front and they would be jostled together in a bleating crowd in a tight place. Yet over the noise, if they would listen—and amazingly, sheep in this situation will listen—they would have heard the noise of a short stout stick, the shepherd's rod, being struck repeatedly against the rock. If they followed the noise they could follow the shepherd's leading without actually seeing him.

What about the shepherd's staff? That was for prodding sheep from behind! It is easier to know the Lord's presence when he prods our conscience or he fixes it so that we have to go where we are being driven. Being able to strain our spiritual ears above the scuffling, jostling and grumbling in the tight place so that we can hear the Lord and know his presence is quite a different art.

Being somewhat claustrophobic, I know how easy it can be to panic in 'tight' places like underground trains, especially if motion stops and the lights go out! But like Jill's experience in the darkness of 'Underland' (*The Silver Chair*) she stayed calm, followed the lights and came out into the sunshine just where Aslan, the Jesus figure in the story, had planned her to. Such knowledge is a comfort and keeps us going.

Are you in a tight place? In silence, ask the Lord to help you hear the sound of the shepherd's rod signalling on the rocky wall of your valley.

Read Hosea 2:15. In every vale of tears there is a door of hope.

AS

Compulsion 3: *Ruach*

Rescue me from my enemies, O Lord, for I hide myself in you. Teach me to do your will, for you are my God; may your good Spirit lead me on level ground.

God's Holy Spirit within us is the power that compels us in our Christian lives. He not only inspires us from without when we feel like fainting and giving up, or calls to us from ahead if we are willing to listen, but lives inside us to motivate us from within. Finding traces of the indwelling Holy Spirit in the psalms is quite difficult, however. In the Old Testament, God's Spirit was not something, or rather someone, that people experienced all the time as an indwelling reality—God's Spirit came and went depending on the spiritual needs or state of the person concerned. The word for God's Spirit was *ruach*, which means 'wind' or 'breath'—it came and went unpredictably. You can see this when David, having sinned, begs God not to take the Holy Spirit away from him (Psalm 51:11) or when Jesus talked to Nicodemus about the Spirit (John 3:5–8).

As Christians we live in a time of a new promise in which the Holy Spirit comes and lives within us continually when we give our lives to God (2 Corinthians 1:22). Amazingly, we can know the presence of the Holy Spirit in a way that was not possible before the Spirit was given at Pentecost as a result of Jesus' death and resurrection (Acts 2). We can know the Holy Spirit compelling us from within. When we are weak, the power of the Spirit within us works with us so that we can do for Christ more than we could ever hope or imagine, and that is the only reason we can state, 'I can do all things in Christ who strengthens me' (Philippians 4:13).

....

Read Psalm 143. Compare David's experience of the Spirit with your own. When we 'hide in God', he is also 'hiding in us'—what difference do you think that makes?

AS

Completion 1: Faithfulness

The Lord is faithful to all his promises and loving towards all he has made. The Lord upholds all those who fall and lifts up all who are bowed down.

We have been looking at four 'signs' that help us remember the Lord's presence in the thick of life's difficulties when it isn't easy to recognize that he is there with us. We have seen he commissioned us, offers companionship and compels us to keep going when we feel like giving up. I have called the final sign 'completion', because the Lord has promised to complete his purposes for all the things he has started—the history of the world and our own personal history.

God's faithfulness is a key characteristic in this respect. Rather like Aslan sending Jill off on her quest in *The Silver Chair*, he wasn't just going to sit on his mountain and forget her; he was faithfully going to ensure the success of the mission within the limits to which Jill was faithful in remembering the signs. In the same way, the Lord doesn't set us a task, ordinary or extraordinary, and then forget about us; he is faithfully there to help us, encourage us, guide us and strengthen us. And when we inevitably make a complete mess of things, he is there to dust us down, forgive us and set us back on the right path. Our part is to be faithful in response to God and to work with him in all the ways we've seen in the past few days, to ensure that our task is finished.

I often panic that I am not going to finish the 'task'—my research project—it seems like an unassailable mountain and the time remaining too short. When that happens, I have to remember that I believe God called me, that he is with me. It's amazing how the right book turns up at the right time—and that he strengthens me when I want to quit.

....

Think about the task God has called you to. Recommit it to him and remember that he is faithful (1 Thessalonians 5:24).

Read Lamentations 3:19–24 and think back on how God has shown his faithfulness to you.

AS

Completion 2: Fulfilment

The Lord will fulfil his purpose for me; your love, O Lord, endures forever—do not abandon the works of your hands.

When we start a project, especially something that will take a considerable length of time, all we can 'see' at the beginning is our own limited version of the complete task somewhere in the distance. What we don't see are the changes that will occur in us as we move from A to B; the person we are when we start out is not the same person who finishes. Along the way we grow and change. These changes in our character are as much the Lord's purpose for us as the completion of the task itself—we are the works of his hands and part of the end result of the task we are set is to mould us more and more into the person he wants us to become.

When Aslan set Jill the task of finding the lost prince, he told her she had to try her hardest to succeed even if it meant dying in the attempt. Of course Jill didn't die—she and her companions found the prince and lived happily ever after. But in one sense Jill did die in the process—all kinds of weaknesses in her character were highlighted and dealt with every time she realized she had failed, admitted her part in the failing and used that moment as an opportunity to grow. The Jill who started the quest was not the same Jill who finished it. But what if she really had died in the process? The strange thing with God is that even what we consider dismal failure can actually be 'fulfilling the task'. All our experiences are redeemable parts of God's plan if we don't allow our hurt pride to complicate the equation. We tend to find later that these experiences are given to us so we can help other people find God in their suffering.

Lord, expand my vision beyond the limited view of a task completed to see your greater purposes in it.

Read Romans 8:28 and think: can you see hidden purposes in your apparent past failures?

AS

Completion 3: Finish

Whoever dwells in the shelter of the Most High will rest in the shadow of the Almighty.

We are promised that the Lord will finish the good work he started in us (Philippians 1:6). That 'good work' however, is the total outcome of God's purposes for the whole of our lives, but completing each task along the way brings us one step nearer to the finish line. At the moment I am mid-life and midway through one of the biggest tasks I have ever taken on besides marriage and child-raising. I think it would be fair to say that I am exhausted and can't wait to cross my short-term finishing line (two years to go) just so I can have a 'rest' before the next thing presents itself.

We do get tired on the way to the finish, but there is a secret to resting in the midst of the busyness of life. This involves all the aspects of the signs to remember along the way that we have been looking at. If we remember who calls, accompanies and compels us then we are able to dwell in the shelter of the Most High and can rest in his shadow, trusting that whatever frustrations the day brings we are more than conquerors because of the Lord's love for us (Romans 8:37).

How much rest we get is not measured by the length of time we spend sitting around doing nothing, but by the state of our relationship with the Lord. The 'rest' we will have in heaven will actually be an 'active', all-consuming relationship with God that occupies every fibre of our being. What makes it restful is the level of spiritual union we will experience with God.

Practising God's presence in this life, growing our trust and assurance in him, will help us know something of that heavenly rest before we cross the short-term and long-term finishing lines.

....

Lord, thank you that you restore my soul with your presence, that your presence is rest. Help me to know that rest every moment.

Read Exodus 33:12–17 and ask yourself: what marks God's people out as different?

AS

Conclusion: Remember

Give thanks to the Lord, call on his name... let the hearts of those who seek the Lord rejoice... Look to the Lord and his strength; seek his face always. Remember the wonders he has done, his miracles, and the judgments he pronounced.

The theme of these notes over the past two weeks has been about remembering what we heard on the mountain top when we were in the Lord's presence, especially when we are down in the valley where the air is thick, making it hard to think straight. We have identified four 'signs' and looked at three aspects of each to help us practise God's presence down there in the thick valley air—the fact he commissioned us, that he is our companion, he compels us and will complete his purposes for our lives.

The last take-home message is not about the 'signs' themselves but about learning to remember them. In *The Silver Chair*, Jill was commanded to rehearse Aslan's signs every morning and every evening so she wouldn't forget them. When she stopped doing this, things very quickly went wrong. Today's reading, Psalm 105, is a song for the people of Israel, helping them to remember and rehearse who God is, what he has promised, what he has done—and to thank him for it.

Every now and then it is a worthwhile exercise for each of us to remember and rehearse where the Lord has brought us from, through what adventures, to get us where we are now and remind ourselves of the reasons we believe God has called us to do the thing we are presently caught up in. It helps get the confusing 'thick air' of the every day out of our heads. Rehearsing his goodness and promises every morning and evening also helps. If you are using *Day by Day with God*, then you are already doing well, but it can help to have a list pinned up of the Lord's special promises that he has made to you—this helps make sure you don't forget the signs and miss the way.

....

'My tongue will tell of your righteous acts all day long, for those who wanted to harm me have been put to shame and confusion' (Psalm 71:24).

Read Psalm 48:14 and commit yourself and the way ahead to the Lord.

AS

Have you noticed God speaking to you over the past few weeks as you have looked at the Psalms? Over these last five days of August, five different women have written about a Bible passage that God has used to speak to them individually. What would you write if you were contributing a page to this series?

Notice how these women approach the Bible. They read it regularly as part of life's daily routine. They expect God to speak. Some read with pen and paper to hand, ready to note action points. Some memorize particularly valuable parts of scripture, focusing on the words that God has seemed to underline and returning to them throughout the day.

What do they find when they read? Encouragement when life seems tough; reassurance that God is at work in their circumstances; guidance as to what steps to take; freedom from condemnation; fresh challenges.

How do you approach the Bible and what do you find as you read? Do you make notes? Underline passages? Memorize verses?

Over these last few days of the month, take time to consider the place the Bible has in your life. These notes are designed to help you to root your life in God's word. Roots hold you up when you are buffeted by life's changing circumstances; if you are rooted, you remain strong and upright whatever happens. Roots provide nourishment, drawing on deep underground reserves; if you are rooted in God's word, your Christian life will grow and flourish. Root systems are rarely seen, but vital; what you learn from God in secret will become evident in your life as you become more like Jesus. In the driest climates, the root system can be much larger than the visible parts of the plant above ground; Christians facing persecution or severe difficulties put down deep roots into God's word. Most types of root do not seek water; they grow where moisture is available. Where there is no water, they remain stunted and the plant might not survive.

Where are you 'rooted' and how healthy is your 'root system'? Get together with others to study God's word. And encourage others to get rooted too! Use the form on page 144 to arrange for a set of these notes to be sent to a friend, then arrange to meet regularly to talk over what God is doing in your lives as you put down roots into his word.

Knowing God in the battle

'Listen… This is what the Lord says to you: "Do not be afraid or discouraged because of this vast army. For the battle is not yours, but God's."'

I am a writer and I'll never forget one day when I was faced with a battle. It was during the week before my deadline to produce a 50,000-word manuscript. I had begun to panic. My battle was against the fear that I wouldn't be able to get my work done on time, or that if I did it wouldn't be good enough. I felt trapped; as if a 'vast army' were coming against me.

That morning I turned to my Bible and read about Jehoshaphat, who had also been 'alarmed' at the battle ahead. But after listening to God, he heard this: 'Do not be afraid or discouraged because of this vast army. For the battle is not yours, but God's' (2 Chronicles 20:15).

The relevance of that story amazed me. I began to study the passage: giving God *more* time to speak to me through his word whereas before, quite honestly, I had come to it hoping I could get my reading done as soon as possible. I began to make notes, to summarize for myself what was relevant. Then I memorized the points of action that the prophet had declared and that I could follow. They were such specific instructions, I could apply them to myself very easily. 'Take up your positions.' For me, that meant, 'Go and sit at your desk!' 'Stand firm and see the deliverance the Lord will give you… Do not be afraid; do not be discouraged. Go out to face them tomorrow, and the Lord will be with you.'

Throughout the day, every time I felt my old fears rising again, I called back into my mind those few words. Each time I did so, the fear receded and I knew that this was from God. He spoke directly into my situation and into my heart.

....

What are you fighting? Can you apply these words and trust God to be with you?

Ephesians 6:13–17 gives more, specific instructions on how you can prepare for battle.

Jane Grayshon

Hearing words and voices

'They will fight against you but will not overcome you, for I am with you and will rescue you,' declares the Lord.

The moment I'd laid eyes on the verses, 'before I formed you in the womb I knew you, before you were born I set you apart', I felt as if the words were aimed directly at me. If I didn't know better, I would've thought someone was in the room with me and talking into my ear.

I didn't know what to think. I was born into a Muslim household, had just converted to Christianity and here was this Bible verse, jumping off the pages and screaming into my ear that God knew about me before I was born and even set me apart for some kind of purpose—going to the nations and preaching or something like that. Was it a fluke? Here I was cowering in fear regarding my conversion, yet here was a Bible verse speaking at me and to me about preaching the gospel and telling me that everything was going to be OK.

I tried to sleep but couldn't. I thought of Jeremiah's life. He was young, afraid that people would not take him seriously as a prophet. In a culture that revered elderly wisdom, he knew many people would not take kindly to his heavenly revelations, yet here was the Lord telling him that he foresaw everything that Jeremiah was going to be, and furthermore, had set him apart for a grand purpose. That relieved my mind immensely. God knew I was going to be born in a Muslim household, he knew I was going to convert, he foresaw everything that would happen in my life and even took time out to have some kind of grand purpose for me. I read on through Jeremiah's life and sighed in relief. He was talking to me through Jeremiah's life. Everything would be fine.

....

Heavenly Father, I know you care for me. You knew me before I was born and set me apart for a reason. Help me to live in the fullness of this knowledge this day and always.

Abidemi Sanusi

God's direction

'I left you in charge of only a little, but now I will put you in charge of much more.'

For two years I had been a group leader at a summer house-party for young people. Then came the phone call. The organizers of the house-party were meeting together to plan the next summer's pro-gramme. One of the senior leaders was unable to continue and a replacement was needed, my name had been mentioned, was I able to take this on? I said I would pray about it and ring back within 24 hours. The responsibilities included supporting two or three group leaders and their team and also being in charge of the house where we stayed.

One of the first things I learnt when I became a Christian is that God really does want to talk to me and will do so in all sorts of ways but primarily through the Bible. This is a book that is alive with God. Not only does it tell me how to live the best life, but, day by day as I read it, God helps me to make good decisions and this was such a case.

In the Bible story, the property owner goes away and leaves his servants in charge of everything. He shares out his money in pro-portion to their abilities, trusting them to do their best for him. When he returns, two of the servants have, with hard work, doubled their money and one has done nothing. The master commends the hardworking servants for being faithful and gives them more responsibility.

The morning after my phone call, this was my Bible reading and I knew that God was pleased with my faithfulness and was giving me more responsibility. This has been a common theme throughout my Christian life that as God sees my faithfulness in small things so I am entrusted with greater things.

....

Remember, for each famous per-son in the world there are mil-lions doing small things faithfully. This is what counts with God.

Read Revelation 21:3–4 to find the ultimate reward for faithfulness.

Caroline Kimber

Don't take off that breastplate!

Stand firm then, with the belt of truth buckled round your waist, with the breastplate of righteousness in place.

'There is someone here who is in turmoil', came the word from the visiting speaker. I knew immediately he was talking about me.

I had unintentionally upset someone who I personally did not know, but who I respected a great deal. I was told of his disquiet about something I had done by a member of our church, who had met him recently. I was horrified! My motive had been for blessing, but it seemed I had been in error. And now, because I had received the rebuke secondhand, I had no way of apologizing or explaining myself. This man's opinion of me was important and even though I had asked the Lord to forgive me, I felt no peace.

The visiting speaker beckoned me out to the front of the church and in prayer lifted off the condemnation and anxiety. Then he spoke a word from the Lord, 'It is I who justifies, and I do not condemn you. Do not take your breastplate off!'

Righteousness is described in this passage as the breastplate because it covers the heart. I learned that Sunday that we can never earn righteousness—it is a free gift from Jesus. No one can give it to us, and to say we don't deserve it is like refusing that precious gift, a gift that cost Jesus everything.

We won't get through this life without making mistakes, consciously or unconsciously and we can never promise we won't sin, or sin again. But that's why Jesus died! He needn't have given up his life on that cross if we could live this life by our own efforts. All we can do is make sure his death isn't wasted, and receive everything it offers us—including forgiveness, righteousness and freedom from condemnation.

....

Are you having trouble receiving forgiveness? Do you feel you don't deserve Jesus' gift of righteousness? Have you taken off your breastplate? Then hear the words of Jesus, 'It is I who justifies and I don't condemn you!'

Mo Tizzard

Bombay blessings

Keep me safe, O God, for in you I take refuge. I said to the Lord, 'You are my Lord; apart from you I have no good thing.'

Bedbugs, cockroaches, 'Delhi belly', peeling paintwork, cracked floor tiles, wire-meshed windows, barking dogs and the unrelenting heat and humidity of 6 a.m. Bombay (now renamed Mumbai) accosted my awakening senses.

Seven months earlier I'd waved goodbye to my cherished island home 4,588 miles away, a loving family, the shattered remnants of a broken relationship and the premature resignation from a promising career. My travels through various countries as a tourist, then short-term missionary, had proved happy and exciting, but on the dawn of my niece's second birthday, my heart throbbed for home. Sitting up in my bunkbed I began reading Psalm 16, but stalled at verse 2, challenged that I could not emulate his sincerity.

I had learnt a lot about God's incomparable goodness through Sunday sermons, midweek Bible studies, Christian literature and recent training at a mission school. Despite this accumulated knowledge, my soul evidently sought solace in the fallible familiarity of home. Hearing or reading about other people's encounters with God had enriched my mind, but only the experience of seeking and engaging with him personally could ever influence the priorities of my heart.

Nothing—not our homes, relationships, work or health—can ever surpass the resultant peace of knowing God's unchanging nature. If, however, we obtain comfort, security or self-worth in temporary objects, fleeting success or imperfect relationships, we run the risk of losing our sense of well-being in an instant. 'Earth has nothing I desire besides you' (Psalm 73:25). Do we truly believe that our relationship with God is the most valuable aspect of our lives? Then let's start digging for treasure!

....

Forgive me, Lord, for the times I've grasped for security in anything but you. I now place myself in the embrace of your everlasting arms.

Read Philippians 3:7–11 and reflect upon Paul's earnest longing to know God, first and foremost, in all situations.

Anne Le Tissier

137

Other Christina Press titles

Women Celebrating Faith edited by Lucinda McDowell (£5.99)
A challenging collection of writings by women from all walks of life, taking time to look back on their lives at forty. No matter what age the reader is, they will be encouraged by the experiences of these women.

Dear God, It's Me and It's Urgent Marion Stroud (£6.99)
The beauty and depth of these prayers for women makes them unforgettable. The fact that they are rooted in everyday life gives them universal appeal.

In His Time Eileen Gordon-Smith (£5.99)
Five missionaries and seven children are killed in a bus crash. Where is God when it hurts? 'I am different now—I no longer fear death.'

Who'd Plant a Church? Diana Archer (£5.99)
Planting an Anglican church from scratch, with a team of four—two adults and two children—is an unusual adventure even in these days. Diana Archer gives a distinctive perspective on parish life.

Pathway Through Grief edited by Jean Watson (£6.99)
Ten Christians, each bereaved, share their experience of loss. Frank and sensitive accounts offering comfort and reassurance to those recently bereaved and new insights to those involved in counselling.

God's Catalyst Rosemary Green (£8.99)
Insight, inspiration and advice for both counsellors and concerned Christians who long to be channels of God's Spirit to help those in need. A unique tool for the non-specialist counsellor.

Angels Keep Watch Carol Hathorne (£5.99)
After 40 years, Carol Hathorne obeyed God's call to Kenya. She came face to face with dangers, hardships and poverty, but experienced the joy of learning that Christianity is still growing in God's world.

Not a Super-Saint Liz Hansford (£6.99)
Describes the outlandish situations that arise in the Manse, where life is both fraught and tremendous fun. A book for the ordinary Christian who feels they must be the only one who hasn't quite got it together.

Other BRF titles

God Has Daughters Too Abidemi Sanusi (£6.99) *Available June 06*
Hear the lives of ten Bible women as you've never heard them before:
their individual battles with family tensions, powerlessness, love and
loss—and their relationship with the God of love, who will not let them
go, no matter how many times they kick against him. The issues and
choices they faced are not so different from those we face today; and
just as they experienced God's grace, so we can experience it at work
in our circumstances, no matter how difficult.

Spirited Women Mary Ellen Ashcroft (£6.99)
An invitation to travel across time and space in order to encounter
lost relatives in the Christian faith. Set during the time of the book of
Acts, just after the death of Stephen, the first martyr, it explores the
stories of some of the women involved in the early Church—Mary
Magdalene, Martha, Mary the mother of Jesus, and Joanna, among
others.

Diary of an (Extra)Ordinary Woman Clare Blake (£6.99)
In this book we share extracts from Clare's diary over the course of a
year—the highs and lows, the everyday challenges and not a few
life-changing experiences. Combined with these episodes are Bible-
based reflections, each one highlighting a particular insight that can
help us as we face similar situations and seek to grow our faith in the
God who can transform us into (extra)ordinary disciples.

Quiet Spaces: The Garden (£4.99)
The fourth issue of BRF's prayer and spirituality journal takes the
theme of the garden, an image that resonates in our hearts because
it has been part of us from the very beginning of creation. The arti-
cles are all linked to this theme in some way, whether literal cele-
brations of caring for the natural world or drawing on related ideas.
We consider how we can still sense his guiding presence us today,
drawing close to us as he once drew close in the 'cool of the day' to
walk and talk with his creatures. The next two issues will be entitled
The Wilderness (July) and *The City* (November).

YOU CAN ORDER THE TITLES ON THESE TWO PAGES FROM CHRISTINA PRESS OR
BRF, USING THE ORDER FORMS ON PAGES 140 AND 141.

Christina Press Publications Order Form

All of these publications are available from Christian bookshops everywhere or, in case of difficulty, direct from the publisher. Please make your selection below, complete the payment details and send your order with payment as appropriate to:

Christina Press Ltd, 17 Church Road, Tunbridge Wells, Kent TN1 1LG

		Qty	Price	Total
8700	God's Catalyst	____	£8.99	____
8701	Women Celebrating Faith	____	£5.99	____
8702	Precious to God	____	£5.99	____
8703	Angels Keep Watch	____	£5.99	____
8704	Life Path	____	£5.99	____
8705	Pathway Through Grief	____	£6.99	____
8706	Who'd Plant a Church?	____	£5.99	____
8707	Dear God, It's Me and It's Urgent	____	£6.99	____
8708	Not a Super-Saint	____	£6.99	____
8709	The Addiction of a Busy Life	____	£5.99	____
8710	In His Time	____	£5.99	____

POSTAGE AND PACKING CHARGES				
	UK	Europe	Surface	Air Mail
£7.00 & under	£1.25	£3.00	£3.50	£5.50
£7.10–£29.99	£2.25	£5.50	£6.50	£10.00
£30.00 & over	free	prices on request		

Total cost of books £ _____
Postage and Packing £ _____
TOTAL £ _____

All prices are correct at time of going to press, are subject to the prevailing rate of VAT and may be subject to change without prior warning.

Name _____

Address _____

_____

_____ Postcode _____

Total enclosed £ _____ (cheques should be made payable to 'Christina Press Ltd')

☐ Please do not send me further information about Christina Press publications

BRF Publications Order Form

All of these publications are available from Christian bookshops everywhere, or in case of difficulty direct from the publisher. Please make your selection below, complete the payment details and send your order with payment as appropriate to:

BRF, First Floor, Elsfield Hall, 15–17 Elsfield Way, Oxford OX2 8FG

		Qty	Price	Total
417 6	God Has Daughters Too	_____	£6.99	_____
443 5	Spirited Women	_____	£6.99	_____
426 5	Diary of an (Extra)Ordinary Woman	_____	£6.99	_____
450 8	Quiet Spaces: The Garden	_____	£4.99	_____
482 6	Quiet Spaces: The Wilderness	_____	£4.99	_____
483 4	Quiet Spaces: The City	_____	£4.99	_____

POSTAGE AND PACKING CHARGES				
	UK	Europe	Surface	Air Mail
£7.00 & under	£1.25	£3.00	£3.50	£5.50
£7.10–£29.99	£2.25	£5.50	£6.50	£10.00
£30.00 & over	free	prices on request		

Total cost of books £ _____
Postage and Packing £ _____
TOTAL £ _____

All prices are correct at time of going to press, are subject to the prevailing rate of VAT and may be subject to change without prior warning.

Name _____

Address _____

_____ Postcode _____

Total enclosed £ _____ (cheques should be made payable to 'BRF')
Payment by: cheque ❏ postal order ❏ Visa ❏ Mastercard ❏ Switch ❏

Card no. ☐☐☐☐☐☐☐☐☐☐☐☐☐☐☐☐☐☐☐

Card expiry date ☐☐☐☐ Issue number (Switch) ☐☐☐☐

Signature _____
(essential if paying by credit/Switch card)

❏ Please do not send me further information about BRF publications

Visit the BRF website at www.brf.org.uk

BRF is a Registered Charity

Subscription Information

Each issue of *Day by Day with God* is available from Christian book-shops everywhere. Copies may also be available through your church Book Agent or from the person who distributes Bible reading notes in your church.

Alternatively you may obtain *Day by Day with God* on subscription direct from the publishers. There are two kinds of subscription:

Individual Subscriptions are for four copies or less, and include postage and packing. To order an annual Individual Subscription please complete the details on page 144 and send the coupon with payment to BRF in Oxford. You can also use the form to order a Gift Subscription for a friend.

Church Subscriptions are for five copies or more, sent to one address, and are supplied post free. Church Subscriptions run from 1 May to 30 April each year and are invoiced annually. To order a Church Subscription please complete the details opposite and send the coupon to BRF in Oxford. You will receive an invoice with the first issue of notes.

All subscription enquiries should be directed to:

BRF
First Floor
Elsfield Hall
15–17 Elsfield Way
Oxford
OX2 8FG

Tel: 01865 319700
Fax: 01865 319701
E-mail: subscriptions@brf.org.uk

Church Subscriptions

The Church Subscription rate for *Day by Day with God* will be £10.80 per person until April 2007.

❏ I would like to take out a church subscription for _____ (Qty) copies.

❏ Please start my order with the September 2006 / January / May 2007* issue. I would like to pay annually/receive an invoice with each edition of the notes*.
(*Please delete as appropriate)

Please do not send any money with your order. Send your order to BRF and we will send you an invoice. The Church Subscription year is from May to April. If you start subscribing in the middle of a subscription year we will invoice you for the remaining number of issues left in that year.

Name and address of the person organising the Church Subscription:

Name _____

Address _____

_____

Postcode _____Telephone _____

Church _____

Name of Minister _____

Name and address of the person paying the invoice if the invoice needs to be sent directly to them:

Name _____

Address _____

_____

Postcode _____Telephone _____

Please send your coupon to:

BRF
First Floor
Elsfield Hall
15–17 Elsfield Way
Oxford
OX2 8FG

❏ Please do not send me further information about BRF publications

DBDWG0206   BRF is a Registered Charity

Individual Subscriptions

❏ I would like to give a gift subscription (please complete both name and address sections below)

❏ I would like to take out a subscription myself (complete your name and address details only once)

Your name _____
Your address _____
_____ Postcode _____

Gift subscription name _____
Gift subscription address _____
_____ Postcode _____

Please send *Day by Day with God* for one year, beginning with the September 2006 / January / May 2007 issue: (delete as applicable)

	UK	Surface	Air Mail
Day by Day with God	❏ £12.75	❏ £14.10	❏ £16.35
2-year subscription	❏ £22.20	N/A	N/A

I would like to take out an annual subscription to *Quiet Spaces* beginning with the next available issue:

	UK	Surface	Air Mail
Quiet Spaces	❏ £16.95	❏ £18.45	❏ £20.85

Please complete the payment details below and send your coupon, with appropriate payment, to BRF, First Floor, Elsfield Hall, 15–17 Elsfield Way, Oxford OX2 8FG

Total enclosed £ _____ (cheques should be made payable to 'BRF')
Payment by: cheque ❏ postal order ❏ Visa ❏ Mastercard ❏ Switch ❏

Card no. ☐☐☐☐☐☐☐☐☐☐☐☐☐☐☐☐☐☐☐☐☐☐

Card expiry date ☐☐☐☐ Issue number (Switch) ☐☐☐☐

Signature _____
(essential if paying by credit/Switch card)

NB: These notes are also available from Christian bookshops everywhere.

❏ Please do not send me further information about BRF publications

DBDWG0206   BRF is a Registered Charity